INTERNATIONAL FOOTBALL BOOK

No. 34

WEMBLEY WONDERS

LIVERPOOL have seen it all before—but there's still nothing to match that victory feeling at wonderful Wembley. And what's the reason for celebration? Another FA Cup triumph, this time 2–0 over Sunderland.

BARCELONA are not new to trophy-winning, but Wembley was the perfect setting for their one-goal defeat of Sampdoria in the 1992 European Cup Final.

INTERNATIONAL FOOTBALL BOOK No. 34

Edited by
Hallam Gordon

SOUVENIR PRESS LTD · LONDON

ISBN 0 285 63064 4

> *All the pictures, including the cover, were taken by AllSport Photographic plc, London SW19*

Filmset and printed in Great Britain
by BAS Printers Limited, Over Wallop, Hampshire.

DUTCH DELIGHT

Celebration time for Ajax on winning the UEFA Cup, even though both legs with Torino ended in a draw. Ajax won on away goals and it's party time here for (left to right) Stanley Menzo (No. 1), Marciano Vink, Aron Winter and Johnny Van't Schip.

Contents

Welcome to

THE 'Year of Europe' was how 1992 was described—a time of economic and political union. But football also played its part in bringing together the different areas of the continent through movement in the transfer market.

The small ranks of British players abroad were boosted by the arrival in Italian football of Paul Gascoigne (£5.5 million from Tottenham to Lazio) and Des Walker (£1.5 million from Nottingham Forest to Sampdoria) in June 1992.

They joined midfielder David Platt, who was a huge success in his first season in Serie A with his

The ABC

GUDNI BERGSSON (Tottenham Hotspur), Iceland, 21.7.65: His versatility made him a vital member of the Tottenham squad. Can play in every defensive position and in midfield. A law student, he has represented his country at every level and made his senior international debut at nineteen. Joined Spurs from Valur Reykjavik in December 1988 after two months on loan.

MATTHIAS BREITKREUTZ (Aston Villa), Germany, 12.5.71: Berlin-born midfielder, spotted by Aston Villa playing for little-known club Bergmann Borsig and signed by the Midlands club in a £125,000 transfer in October 1991. Made his debut in January 1992 and enjoyed a regular run in the side towards the end of the season, impressing with his skill and vision.

ERIC CANTONA (Leeds), France, 24.5.66: Known as *enfant terrible* in France after numerous scrapes with his country's football authorities. Disillusioned at Nimes, he retired but returned later that season, February 1992, with Sheffield Wednesday on trial. Then joined Leeds on loan and helped them secure the League title. Moved to Elland Road in a permanent £900,000 deal in May 1992.

Britain

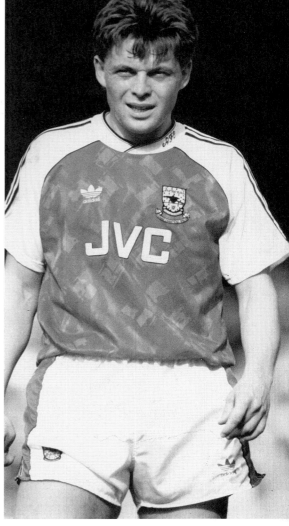

brilliant displays for a struggling Bari side before his lucrative move to Juventus.

The remainder of British stars abroad were stationed in France. Trevor Steven and Chris Waddle were key members of the Marseille side which won the French League title, while former Arsenal midfielder Graham Rix completed his fourth season with Caen.

British football, by contrast, has become laden with foreign talent. Here is an ABC of some of the players who lit up the domestic scene in 1992, presented by JOHN PRICE.

# of talent

DARIUSZ DZIEKANOWSKI (Bristol City), Poland, 30.9.62: Striker, formerly with Widzew Lodz and Legia Warsaw, he moved to Celtic in 1989 and became a firm favourite with the Parkhead fans but struggled for consistency due to a series of injuries. Did not figure in the plans of new Celtic manager Liam Brady and joined Bristol City for £250,000 in January 1992.

ANDREJ KANCHELSKIS (Manchester United), CIS, 23.1.69: This Ukranian made an immediate impact with the Manchester United supporters with his surging runs and powerful shooting. A bargain £650,000 buy in April 1991 from Shakhtyor Donetsk, he formed a potent wing-to-wing partnership with young Welshman Ryan Giggs as United won the Rumbelows Cup.

ISTVAN KOZMA (Liverpool), Hungary, 3.12.64: Liverpool paid Dunfermline £300,000 for him in February 1992 to bolster their injury-hit squad. Made a couple of appearances in their FA Cup run but did not play in the 2–0 Final win over Sunderland. A midfielder, he started at Ujpest Dozsa and had a spell with Bordeaux, of France, before his move to Scotland.

ABOVE Paal Lydersen in Arsenal shirt, making his debut six months after signing from Norwegian club Start.

OPPOSITE Eric Cantona was an instant hit with Leeds fans after his "retirement" in France.

Kanchelskis the Ukranian
played a vital role in
Manchester United's 1992
Rumbelows Cup victory.

DARIUSZ KUBICKI (Aston Villa), Poland, 6.6.63: Warsaw-born full-back who is as good in attack as he is in defence. Won league and cup honours in Poland with Legia Warsaw and came to the attention of Villa manager Ron Atkinson with his impressive performances against England in the qualifiers for the 1990 World Cup. Joined Villa for £200,000 in July 1991.

OLEG KUZNETSOV (Rangers), CIS, 2.3.63: This central defender lifted every domestic honour with Dynamo Kiev and joined Rangers for a £1.4 million fee in October 1990. Injured in only his third game for Rangers, he was out of the game for nearly a year but returned to help the Ibrox club to their fourth successive Premier League title in 1992.

ANDERS LIMPAR (Arsenal), Sweden, 24.9.65: Has established himself as one of the most popular players at Arsenal with his delightful skills on either wing. Signed for £1 million from Italian club Cremonese in July 1991, he contributed eleven goals towards the Gunners' Championship success in his first season at the club.

PAAL LYDERSEN (Arsenal), Norway, 10.9.65: Signed by Arsenal for his ability to fill every defensive position, including sweeper. Cost the Gunners £500,000 from Norwegian club Start in September 1991 but had to wait for another six months before making his Arsenal debut.

ALEXEI MIKHAILICHENKO (Rangers), CIS, 22.3.63: An attacking mid-fielder, he contributed twelve goals as Rangers won their first League and Cup 'double' for fourteen years in 1992. Previously won the Soviet and Italian Championships with Dynamo Kiev and Sampdoria respectively. Rangers signed him for £2 million from Sampdoria in July 1991.

LUDEK MIKLOSKO (West Ham), Czechoslovakia, 9.12.61: Regarded as one of the top three goalkeepers in England by West Ham manager Billy Bonds. Was outstanding as the Hammers won promotion to Division One in 1991 but even his brilliance failed to prevent them going down a year later. Cost West Ham £300,000 from Banik Ostrava in January 1990.

JAN MOLBY (Liverpool), Denmark, 4.7.63: This midfielder showed why he is rated as the best passer of the ball in English football with an outstanding display in Liverpool's FA Cup Final win over Sunderland in 1992. Joined Liverpool for £225,000 from Ajax Amsterdam in August 1984 and has also won League title honours with the Merseyside club.

KENNETH MONKOU (Chelsea), Holland, 29.11.64: Born in Surinam, the same place as Dutch international captain Ruud Gullit. A former model, this 6ft 3in central defender moved to Chelsea from Feyenoord in a £100,000 transfer in March 1989. Was voted the London club's 'Player of the Year' in 1990.

NAYIM (Tottenham Hotspur), Spain, 5.11.66: Midfielder whose full name is Mohammed Ali Amar. Moroccan-born, he came from Barcelona for £300,000 in 1989 in a twin transfer with Gary Lineker. Played in Spurs' FA Cup winning side of 1991 and was one of the few consistent players in the London side's disappointing League form the following season.

ROLAND NILSSON (Sheffield Wednesday), Sweden, 27.11.63: Right-back whose overlapping runs were a feature of Sheffield Wednesday's attacking approach as they finished third in Division One to secure a UEFA Cup place in 1992. Joined Wednesday for £375,000 from Gothenburg in December 1989 and was a member of the Yorkshire side which won the 1991 Rumbelows Cup.

THORVALDUR ORLYGSSON (Nottingham Forest), Iceland, 2.8.66: Born in Denmark, this winger is qualified to play for Iceland. Was training to be a lawyer when Nottingham Forest paid KA Akureyri £175,000 for him in December 1989. Has spent the majority of his time at Forest in the reserves but impressed when he broke into the side in the last month of the 1991–92 season.

MIXU PAATELAINEN (Aberdeen), Finland, 3.2.67: This striker spent eleven months in the Finnish Army before starting his career with Valkeakoski Haka. Moved to Dundee United in 1988 after a two-week trial and scored thirty-three Premier League goals for the Tannadice club, joining Aberdeen in a £300,000 transfer in March 1992.

PETER SCHMEICHEL (Manchester United), Denmark, 18.11.63: This 6ft 5in goalkeeper, regarded as the best in Europe by United manager Alex Ferguson, kept twenty-five clean sheets in fifty-four matches to help his club win the Rumbelows League Cup and finish second in the League. United bought him for what now looks like a bargain £600,000 from Brondby in August 1991.

HANS SEGERS (Wimbledon), Holland, 30.10.61: Adventurous goalkeeper who could almost be described as a 'keeper/sweeper! Has been known to go up for corners and free-kicks in the opponents' penalty area when Wimbledon have been behind in the dying minutes of a game. Cost Wimbledon £125,000 in September 1988 from Nottingham Forest, having started with PSV Eindhoven.

THEO SNELDERS (Aberdeen), Holland, 7.12.63: Inspirational goalkeeper who joined Aberdeen from FC Twente for a £300,000 fee in the summer of 1988. Was voted Scotland's PFA 'Player of the Year' in his first season in the Premier Division. Helped the Dons to a Scottish Cup and League Cup 'double' in season 1989–90.

A model at the Bridge

One of Chelsea's most popular defenders, Kenneth Monkou, spent his spare time as a male model before moving to London from Holland.

JAN STEJSKAL (Queens Park Rangers), Czechoslovakia, 15.1.62: Agile 6ft 3in goalkeeper, he moved to Queens Park Rangers from Sparta Prague for £625,000 in October 1990 after his impressive showing in the 1990 World Cup in Italy. Made a nervous start to his career at Loftus Road but has quickly developed into one of the best 'keepers in the English game.

ERIC THORSTVEDT (Tottenham Hotspur), Norway, 31.10.62: This 6ft goalkeeper cost Tottenham £400,000 from Swedish club Gothenburg in December 1988. Played a key role in Tottenham's 1991 FA Cup win over Nottingham Forest. Began with home-town club Viking Stavanger and also had a spell in the Bundesliga with Borussia Moenchengladbach.

GUDMUNDOR TORFASON (St. Mirren), Iceland, 13.12.61: The top scorer with eight goals for St. Mirren in 1991–92, but it was not enough to save them from relegation to Division One. The 6ft 1in striker moved to St. Mirren from RSC Genk in 1989 and his performances for the Love Street side attracted interest from big clubs in both England and Scotland.

ROBERT WARZYCHA (Everton), Poland, 20.8.63: Powerful midfielder, he quickly made an impression for Everton, scoring on his first Wembley appearance for the club in the 1991 Zenith Data Systems Cup Final defeat by Crystal Palace. Signed for Everton from Gornik Zabrze in a £500,000 transfer in March 1991.

Moroccan-born Nayim of Spurs puts in a telling challenge as Chelsea skipper Andy Townsend races through in this London derby.

GOODBYE...
and thanks
to Cloughie

SAYS DES WALKER

ALL things are possible when a footballer is blessed with pace, as England's Des Walker has proved in a meteoric rise to stardom.

In 1982 at the age of sixteen, Walker was down and out at White Hart Lane where Spurs saw little future for the gawky, long-haired youngster who some perceived as having an attitude problem. Walker has always denied this but freely admits that it needed the unique managerial talents of Brian Clough to bring out the best in him.

Walker is now one of the most accomplished defenders on the World scene. A two-year contract with Italian giants Sampdoria has guaranteed England's centre-back an income of £3 million over those two years, plus the not insignificant matter of a £1 million signing-on fee.

Sporting stars are traditionally coy about their earnings but it wouldn't be wildly inaccurate to assume that Walker is the highest-paid defender in the Italian League, with possibly only Franco Baresi contesting the issue.

Walker has swapped his Porsche for a Ferrari and lives in the plush Genoan suburbs of Nervi, where Sampdoria's popular British stars of seasons past— Trevor Francis, Graeme Souness and Liam Brady—have found an idyllic refuge from the intense pressure that is an integral part of Italian football.

Prior to his Italian venture Walker had gone to great lengths to avoid the

Lineker says: I've never seen a finer man-to-man marker

That was the tribute by England's superstar to Des Walker, seen here in action for Nottingham Forest shortly before moving off to Sampdoria.

limelight; indeed he carefully cultivated a 'Garbo' type image which made press interviews as rare as his goals. But nobody can survive in the goldfish bowl of Italian football without co-operating with the Italian media and the excitement of moving to Sampdoria certainly seems to have loosened his tongue.

'I have always kept away from publicity—it's the way I am,' said Walker on his arrival in Italy. 'I prefer not to become the subject of public attention. I enjoy football very much but that's all I want out of it.

'I am here in Italy for the challenge. With the exception of Gary Lineker, the Italians have gathered all the world's top strikers in their league and I want to play against them and see just how good I am. I have always tried to better myself in life—that's what my entry into Italian football is all about.'

Walker was first linked to an Italian club following his superb performances for England in the 1990 World Cup, after which Juventus came in with a reported £3 million bid. He was tempted but decided he wasn't quite ready and that he owed Forest two more years.

He did, however, persuade Forest to insert a clause in his contract restricting his price if he moved abroad. 'It was a present to Des from Cloughie,' explains Walker's agent and friend Dennis Roach. 'It was a reward for his staying with Forest for ten years and being their best player during that time.'

Walker displayed a similar maturity by signing initially for two years at Sampdoria, who were keen to commit their man to a four-year contract. When his contract runs out in 1994 he will still be only twenty-eight and can either re-negotiate a contract with the club or listen to alternative offers.

Although confident of his ability to flourish in the World's best league, Walker is mindful of the British players who have found it tough going abroad and has sensibly given himself the opportunity to reassess the situation in two years' time. One detects the shrewd influence of Brian Clough in the canny way he has conducted himself—and indeed Clough has been a major influence throughout his career.

'I owe a great deal to Nottingham Forest and Brian Clough,' admits Walker. 'They took me as a sixteen-year-old from school and Cloughie has made a major impact on my life and career. He doesn't ask for anything special—he just asks for respect and, if you give it, you get it back. He taught me how to conduct myself like a human being.

'He always knew about my ambition to play in Italy and he left the final decision to me without applying any pressure.'

Walker can reflect on a career of high achievement with Forest, whom he joined as an apprentice in 1982 before signing professional a year later. He made his first-team debut against Everton in March 1984 and has simply got better and better. He won the Nottingham Forest Player of the Year award in 1985–86 and was soon a regular in the England Under-21 side.

Such was Walker's progress that many critics thought he should have been in England's full side for the 1988 European Championship, but Bobby Robson opted for the greater experience of Mark Wright and Terry Butcher. Walker's

chance was soon to come and, by the 1992 European Championship in Sweden, he was an integral part of the England set-up and approaching fifty caps.

On the domestic front he has tasted both ecstasy and agony with Forest at Wembley, twice playing in Littlewoods Cup winning sides but scoring an own goal in their FA Cup defeat against Spurs in 1991 and again receiving a loser's medal in the 1992 Rumbelows Cup Final against Manchester United.

Walker's England colleague Gary Lineker is a fully paid-up member of the Des Walker fan club. 'I've certainly never seen a finer man-to-man marker,' says England's experienced striker, 'and I say that after the experience of three seasons in Spain, where they know quite a bit about defensive play, and a long international career.

'I remember the first time I came up against Des. I was scoring lots of goals for Everton and wasn't too worried by the 'unknown' teenager I read about in the match programme. It took exactly ninety minutes to revise my opinions!

'He isn't a giant but he has terrific 'spring' and can leap high to reach any ball thumped into the penalty area. His timing is immaculate and when he goes into a tackle he invariably stays on his feet. On the rare occasions he is beaten, Dessie has such good powers of recovery that he usually catches the attacker who has managed to slip past.

'On top of all that, he has an excellent temperament, doesn't get involved in any nonsense and always concentrates on the job in hand.'

High praise indeed from a man who has played against the best defenders in the World. Sampdoria's massive investment may yet prove to be a real bargain.

TOP LEFT Des Walker in England action against Renato of Brazil. 'Des isn't a giant but he has terrific spring' says Lineker.
TOP RIGHT Brian Clough, as ever on the touchline, 'has made a major impact on my life and career' says Walker.

Marazola

He's the reluctant hero of Napoli in Diego's shirt

By HARRY PRATT *(Hayters)*

WHEN Diego Maradona eventually made his dramatic exit from Italian football, the player entrusted with the Argentinian's number ten shirt at Napoli was never likely to find life easy. Yet despite pleas not to be compared with the world's most recently acclaimed footballer, Gianfranco Zola has already earned the nickname 'Marazola'.

The quiet, unassuming striker, who was born at Oliena in the north-east of Sardinia on July 5, 1966, has well deserved the accolades that have flowed his way. Quite simply, he has helped to transform the fortunes of Napoli.

The loss of Maradona in March 1991 appeared a catastrophic blow for the club which had become a major force in Italian football. In seven superb seasons with Maradona, Napoli had won their first two League titles, the Italian Cup and the UEFA Cup.

With his departure, predictions were rife that there would be no way back into the top flight of European football for Napoli. At the time they were struggling with twenty-five points and goals from twenty-six games. Without his destabilising influence, however, the resurgence began. Napoli were unbeaten in their final eight games of the 1990–91 season and finished eighth in the League.

Even so, the club faced worrying statistics. At the start of the following season, ticket sales had fallen by two-thirds and clearly the loss of Maradona's extrovert style and charisma was the reason. The solution was soon forthcoming, however, with Zola emerging as the exciting replacement for their

Both eyes on the ball and in perfect control in his star role for Napoli, Zola is now amply repaying his club for their patience with him.

fallen idol. Gates gradually rose to 50,000 and beyond, and their qualifying for the UEFA Cup by finishing third behind Milan and Juventus rightly reflected the team's improvement.

Zola, by contrast to Maradona, does not court publicity. In the past, few Sardinians have emerged to become stars of Italian football, but Zola had won three international caps by the end of the 1991–92 season and was clearly heading for wealth and fame.

Zola's career first began to take shape in April 1989 when Luciano Moggi, then general manager of Napoli, was invited by his Torres counterpart,

Valentino Barbanera, to watch a player he believed to be too good for the Italian Fourth Division.

Barbanera's judgement was vindicated when, two months later, Zola was on his way to the mainland to join Napoli. The potential had always been there according to Giovanni Maria Mele, the coach of Zola's hometown club Sassari. 'I wasn't wrong about him back in 1980,' says Mele. 'He was only tiny then but enormously gifted. A real little champion.'

Mele's only concern was that Zola's physique may not be sufficient to withstand the demanding nature of Italian football. So Zola was placed on an arduous training schedule.

Mele comments: 'I placed my trust in Nardinu Masu, an ex-Olympian and coach of the national weightlifting team. Gianfranco worked very hard with Masu, although the workouts would often reduce him to tears. I had to keep reminding him that one day he would play for Italy.'

Eating masses of junk food enabled Zola to increase his body size and while at Torres he gained the nickname 'Merendina' (*meaning snack*) because he consumed such a vast amount of biscuits.

A £300,000 fee, plus three youth players, was enough to take Zola to Napoli, but for two years he was no more than a reserve waiting on the subs' bench. But Zola was far from frustrated at the lack of opportunity and he dedicated every moment to studying the technique and style of Maradona. 'I learned a great deal from Diego,' says Zola. 'To work so closely with the greatest player in the world is an experience every player should share.'

During 1990, it appeared that Zola would be sold after Fiorentina and Lecce had expressed interest in the reserve striker, but Napoli president Corrado Ferlaino rejected the inquiries. Says Zola: 'I have to thank the president and my team-mates who have always helped me, even when my departure seemed a certainty. I always knew that in this profession there would be highs and lows. I never gave in because I was sure that, sooner or later, my opportunity would come.' He has taken the chance with verve and so prominent has he been that Napoli have signed him on a new contract until 1994.

Who else but the great little man himself, Diego Maradona? He made Napoli a truly great club, says Zola.

'I feel very comfortable here and I could happily stay for the rest of my career,' says this generous and thoughtful man who, despite all the trappings of success, remains true to his principles.

Zola agrees there can never be another Maradona, but he believes that Napoli can once again make a realistic challenge to the supremacy of the Italian giants Juventus, AC Milan and Sampdoria.

'I don't believe titles are won solely on the strength of the number of players a club acquires,' he says. 'Of course they have an advantage, but it does not necessarily promise success. Although here we cannot compete with Milan or Juventus in the transfer market, we are able to challenge them through sheer hard work and by maintaining our professionalism.

'We all work for each other, but we will still need to grow if we are to reach the heights of Diego's era—and, in particular, me. He made this a truly great club. I haven't . . . yet.'

Presenting the big red book . . . Stephen Davies

THIS IS YOUR LIFE . . .

ONCE a PE teacher and Third Division footballer, he rose from managing non-League Boston United to winning the most prized possession in the English game—The First Division title. Now, International Football Book salutes Howard Wilkinson, manager of Leeds United, by saying . . . This Is Your Life!

HOWARD WILKINSON

YOU were born Howard Wilkinson in Sheffield on November 13, 1943, and from an early age it was clear that you had set your sights on football as a career. 'That's right. At the age of six or seven I'd decided I wanted to be a footballer.'

There was sufficient promise to earn a contract with Sheffield Wednesday when you were eighteen, but after making fewer than thirty appearances on the wing for the local club you dropped into the Third Division with Brighton in 1966. It soon dawned on you that there might be a better option to playing.

'Yes, it was at an early point in my career that I decided I would prefer management. I wasn't getting what I wanted out of football in the Third Division so I turned to coaching more or less as a way of killing time. To my surprise I found I was good at it.'

To such an extent, in fact, that you were awarded your FA badge at the age of twenty-four and worked as a player-coach with Boston while gaining a Bachelor of Education degree at Sheffield University.

You won three Northern Premier League titles in a six-year spell as player-manager with Boston before the FA appointed you a regional coach and then you became manager of the England semi-professional team.

It was at a coaching course in 1979 that you were approached by Notts County manager *JIMMY SIRRELL*, who wanted you to assist in coaching the first team at Meadow Lane, something that gave you reservations.

'My initial reaction was to say "You've got to be joking". Jimmy was the sort of manager who did everything and I didn't want to be the man who just carried balls to training. I told him I'd only take the job if he promised to keep away from the training ground and, to my astonishment, he agreed.'

Besides Jimmy, there was another man who knew you were right for the job—Notts County's chief executive *NEAL HOOK*.

'We did wonder who this regional coach was who was joining us. But as soon as you met Howard you felt he was a man heading for the top. He was supremely confident, a hard task-master, but the players responded to him straight away.'

Your first season at Meadow Lane ended with promotion to the First Division. In June 1983, while managing the England Under-21s on a part-time basis, you turned down a three-year contract at Notts County and the job as Bobby Robson's right-hand man with England to take over Second Division Sheffield Wednesday. Why?

'Hillsborough holds 50,000 and it's a marvellous sight when it is full. I'm a fairly clinical thinker but managing Wednesday was a job that stirred my emotions. I saw my first game at Hillsborough perched on my father's shoulders and I remember how excited I was when they took me on as a player.'

In a little over five years in charge of Wednesday you guided them into the First Division but on October 10, 1988, you left to become manager of Leeds United, a side struggling near the foot of the Second Division.

Your ability at buying and then motivating players, though, held you in good stead. One of the bargains of recent years was signing *GORDON STRACHAN* from Manchester United for £300,000 in March 1989.

The Scottish midfielder had appeared to be on his way to modest French club Lens until you brought him to Elland Road. Gordon sensed you were perhaps being slightly optimistic in predicting that a club facing relegation to the Third Division could be in the First Division within two seasons.

'Howard told me that it would take a year. I had a look round and thought it would take three or four years. My ambition was to get Leeds back into the First Division but winning the championship so soon is a tribute to Howard as a manager.'

Leeds avoided relegation and were crowned Second Division champions in

Gordon Strachan was one of Wilkinson's inspired signings, from Manchester United for a mere £300,000. He was a proud skipper in Leeds' dramatic Championship year.

'The first part of my greatest football ambition'

Howard Wilkinson holds high the Barclays League Division One Championship trophy for 1992. Now his dream will come true the day Leeds win the European Cup!

May 1990—just as you had predicted they would be. And you strengthened the team still further with more excellent signings. Midfielder Gary McAllister came from Leicester and goalkeeper John Lukic from Arsenal, each for £1 million, while central defender Chris Whyte from West Brom was a snip at £450,000.

Leeds finished fourth on their return to the First Division and in the summer of 1991 you continued the relentless drive towards honours with more important signings, such as left-back Tony Dorigo from Chelsea for £1.3 million and Rod Wallace from Southampton for £1.6 million.

From early in the season, it was clear that this Leeds side was capable of winning the club's first Football League Championship since 1974 and the magical days of Don Revie.

The title was a two-horse race between yourselves and Manchester United, and when you won at Sheffield United and Manchester United lost to Liverpool on the penultimate weekend of the season, you had achieved your dream.

After that 3–2 win at Bramall Lane had been followed by Liverpool's victory over your closest rivals, you said: 'This is the first part of my greatest football ambition. Ever since I went into management at the age of twenty-eight, I dreamt of winning the title and then the European Cup. But I was young and stupid in those days and I recognised later that when people got into politics they don't automatically become Prime Minister.'

Your closest ally at the club is chairman *LESLIE SILVER*, a man who has allowed you to buy the necessary players whatever the cost and he wants you to realise your dream. 'Our debt to Howard is enormous. It was his calmness and style of management that carried us through. He is now on a contract that will keep him at Leeds for as long as he wants to be manager of a football club.'

And who is to say what might be achieved over the coming years? Howard Wilkinson—This Is Your Life!

Leeds left-back Tony Dorigo was a vital signing in the construction of a Championship-winning squad. He cost a cool £1.3 million from Chelsea in the summer of 1991.

WAS IT REALLY 25 YEARS AGO?

LIAM BRADY in pensive mood talking to Damon Quigley (*Sunday Times*)

FOR just a few brief, nostalgic hours of May 1992, Celtic supporters everywhere put the disappointment of another trophy-less season behind them in order to celebrate the twenty-fifth anniversary of the club's 1967 European Cup Final win against Inter Milan. Those who had been involved in that unforgettable Lisbon occasion returned to the public eye to be lionised once more, and few could believe that so many years had passed since Jock Stein had taken Celtic to the pinnacle of world football.

As far as most Celtic fans were concerned, however, it seemed as likely to be many more years before they could hope for anything resembling a repeat of their most significant achievement. Yet, only twelve months earlier, the East End of Glasgow had seen the promise of a new era as former Republic of Ireland midfielder, Liam Brady, became only the seventh man to manage the club.

Whether they like it or not, Old Firm managers are judged largely by the measure of dominance they achieve in the city rivalry and, in that respect, Brady's first season was somewhat inconclusive. The bare statistics were unimpressive—three defeats, one draw and a solitary victory—but they do not tell the whole story.

On a glorious late August afternoon, the Glasgow giants met for the first time since Brady's appointment and, with home advantage, the expectations of the Celtic fans were high. Had not Rangers been humbled twice in seven days on their most recent visits to Celtic Park? The new manager's honeymoon period was decisively ended by two Mark Hateley goals. 'That just showed that we were a long way behind Rangers and that it would take an awful lot of hard work to catch up,' Brady admitted.

In November, Tony Cascarino scored one of the few goals of his brief Celtic career to earn a draw at Ibrox, and by the time of the traditional New Year's Day encounter, both teams knew that the result would be pivotal in the title race. Having fallen behind just before halftime, Celtic equalised through Tony Mowbray and, with Paul McStay performing majestically in midfield, seemed likely winners. When McStay was forced to leave the field with a facial cut, however, the momentum was lost and a disputed penalty set Rangers en route to a crucial triumph.

The collapse of Celtic's Premier Division championship ambitions was a severe blow to the club, but Brady kept faith with a patient, passing style which some regarded as incompatible with the raw physical nature of the Scottish game. The Irishman was vindicated by a run of sixteen league matches without defeat.

That included Celtic's first win on Rangers' territory since 1988, and even more encouraging was the manner of their 2–0 success. 'I think the fact that we were able to go there and win so well was an indication of how much progress we had made,' said Brady.

Ten days later, however, it was a different story. Celtic had beaten the Ibrox side in the Scottish Cup in each of the three previous seasons, but Rangers survived the early dismissal of David Robertson and a second half in which Celtic thrice struck the woodwork to advance to the cup final.

'That was a big disappointment,' said Brady, 'because I really believed we could win a trophy in my first season and we were certainly playing well enough at that stage. On that particular night, however, we were too naive. We played timidly when Rangers were reduced to ten men after only six minutes, and then they scored right on the halftime whistle. We were much better in the second half, but fortune just wasn't smiling on us. Having said that, you had to give credit to Rangers for some remarkably resilient defending.'

A calamitous defeat in their final league match against Hibernian seemed to have deprived Brady's team of even a UEFA Cup place, but they were given a post-season reprieve when the European football authorities created an extra space in that competition. That represented perhaps the first piece of genuine good fortune to have befallen the club in recent years. Indecision over a new stadium and lack of on-field success had put Celtic into a downward spiral since their 1988 Centenary year League and Cup double.

If ever a club needed a break it was Celtic, but Brady is determined that his players will make their own good luck from now on. 'It was important, because a club like Celtic should always be in Europe, and it gave us a fresh challenge for the new season, even though I would have preferred to have earned the place by our own efforts.'

While the Celtic manager cannot hope to follow Rangers' high-spending

Celtic Park heroes old and new

Gerry Creaney (left) has already been picked for Scotland Under-21 side. Now he hopes to emulate the great Celtic man before him, Kenny Dalglish (below).

Charlie Nicholas has endeared himself to the Celtic fans with his skills and goalscoring knack, but there have been problems along the way. This wee exchange with the ref, for example.

policy in pursuit of domestic and European glory, he feels he can blend some more modest purchases with the latest generation of home-bred talent. Brian O'Neil, Gerry Creaney and Mark McNally have already established themselves as first-team players at Celtic Park, as well as appearing with distinction in the Scotland Under-21 team. They promise to be worthy successors to Billy McNeil, Kenny Dalglish, Charlie Nicholas and Paul McStay, some of the most notable players the club has produced since the war.

'I think over the next few years, the Celtic team will have a young look about it,' said Brady. 'We were able to introduce the likes of Brian O'Neil, Mark Donaghy and Barry Smith to the first team in the 1991–92 season and, hopefully, that will give other lads encouragement. Age certainly doesn't matter to me.'

Many of those who will wear the famous hooped jerseys in the coming seasons will probably not have been born when Billy McNeill became the first Briton to lift the European Cup. Their task, therefore, is to write their own chapter in the Celtic history books.

Pele beats the drum for Africa

By NICK CALLOW *(News of the World)*

A PROFESSIONAL footballer has to be very good, verging on the exceptional, if he is to make his way under the name Pele. Fortunately for him, the latest pretender to the great Brazilian crown is just that.

Ghanaian Abedi Ayew, known universally as Pele, is the key to Marseille's tilt at becoming Europe's finest club side and heads a rich crop of African talent competing in Europe. Unfortunately for him, he has bewildered as many managers as he has opponents with his agile dribbling, first-time flicks, explosive shooting power and pursuit of excellence.

At seventeen, Pele appeared in the 1982 African Nations Cup, but ten years elapsed before he featured in a European Cup final, playing at his best. After a fruitless spell in the Middle East and an equally barren stay with Dragons of Benin, Pele was taken to Zurich. Even then his in-and-out form impressed only lowly French side Niort.

Yet France represented a chance to make a name and, after he had scored fourteen goals in his first season, the big boys moved in. St Etienne, Paris

St Germain and German giants Bayern Munich all took Pele on trial, but they all let him go. Finally, big-spending Marseille signed him.

Would the world now sit up and take note of the African wizard? No. Pele had a miserable time and there were reports of training-ground fisticuffs with the No. 1 striker Jean-Pierre Papin. If you did not get on with Papin, you did not get on with Marseille . . . so it was off to another French club, Lille.

In the relaxed atmosphere of a mid-table side, Pele again let his football do the talking and waited for the big clubs to marvel at his feet. Yet the managers and agents, who decide who plays where and with whom, negotiated once more and, against his better judgment, Pele was back with Marseille.

This time, with a new coach, Raymond Goethals, and a new star, Chris Waddle, acting as the buffer against Papin, Pele revelled in his new free role and inspired Marseille to the 1991 European Cup Final, in which they were beaten on penalties by Red Star Belgrade.

Another good season took him into 1992 as Africa's Player of the Year with 206 votes in the poll organised by the Paris-based magazine *African Football*. In second place was Monaco's George Weah from Liberia, the 1990 winner who polled 146 votes. Another Ghanaian, Nii Lamptey, the teenage protégé of Anderlecht, was third with 68 votes.

World attention turned towards African football after Cameroon's spectacular contribution to the 1990 World Cup in Italy. There are now eighteen Cameroonians playing in Europe.

By the start of the 1991–92 season, more than 100 of the 250-plus African players in Europe were involved in the French League, there were fifty-six in Belgium and forty-eight in Portugal. Italy and Spain remained unconvinced and had none.

In England there was a spurious ten, including, in the First Division, Zimbabwean goalkeeper Bruce Grobbelaar at Liverpool; Sierra Leone's, but Middlesbrough-born, Chris Kamara at Leeds; John Salako of Nigeria, at Crystal Palace; and QPR reserve team forward, Nigerian Dominic Iorfa. The rest were either white South Africans or playing with relatively nondescript sides from the lower reaches of the lower divisions.

French and Portuguese teams have been importing African players since the 1950s and there are few more famous African exports than Mozambique-born Eusebio, who lit up Benfica's Stadium of Light with his dazzling skills in the 1960s.

These days the star names are Lamptey, the Ghanaian who has swept all before him in Belgium, and Soulemane Sane, a regular scorer in the German Bundesliga. Dutch champions PSV Eindhoven have Kalusha Bwalya, the key to Zambia's international side.

Nigeria is the biggest supplier of players with thirty-five earning their way in Europe and it is a trade which has left them with fewer internationals playing at home than there are abroad. Now, most African nations can lay claim to stars in Europe.

The future of this growth industry depends largely on the success of African

Abedi Pele . . . 'inspired Marseille to the European Cup Final'

ABOVE Happiness here is a man called John Salako, a splendid signing by Crystal Palace before he was laid low by a crippling injury.

OPPOSITE It's that extrovert gentleman goalkeeper Bruce Grobbelaar of Zimbabwe and Liverpool, seen here defying Sunderland raiders in the 1992 FA Cup Final.

teams at international level and there was no shortage of European scouts and managers at the African Nations Cup, held at the start of 1992.

That should have been Pele's greatest stage to date. He was voted the player of the tournament and Ghana reached the final. Two bookings, however, the second coming in the semi-final win over Tunisia, meant that Pele had to watch his team-mates go down in a nerve-wracking 11–10 penalty shoot-out to the Ivory Coast.

Afterwards, Pele plotted the way forward for African football when he said: 'To develop, we must marry the best of African skill with the organisation and training and coaching of the European game. Only then will we progress. That is what Brazil have had to do. So now Africa is no different. If we want to prove worthy of hosting World Cups and winning international tournaments, that must be the right way to go.'

It will be a shame if the attacking talents of the African game are sacrificed for Europe's deadly grip on placing results ahead of entertainment. It would also be unfair to cast the same die over the whole of African football—that is like describing English, Italian, French and German football in the same vein.

Different footballing styles and concepts in Africa depend on the diversities of geography, culture, economic climates and heritage. Tunisia, the first African nation to record a World Cup win when they beat Mexico in the 1978 World Cup, are from the powerful Maghreb region, which covers north-west Africa. It is credited as being the most technically advanced African region, with its proximity to Europe and close links with France. Here, the footballer as an artiste is held in the highest esteem.

In Egypt, Africa's oldest soccer-playing nation, they adopt a more cautious defence-orientated style of play and discourage wanton creativity.

The West African game is split between English and French influences, but that has resulted in the likes of Senegal and the Ivory Coast finding it difficult to harness the two philosophies into one winning style.

Pele is a rare exception in a land of big English-style centre-forwards favoured by the West African countries like Nigeria and Ghana. Only the Cameroonians seem to have blended successfully the Anglo-French attributes and, as seen in the World Cup, have that other essential ingredient—luck!

In the South, Zambia have had their football heavily fashioned by a succession of British managers from Bill McGarry to Danny McGrain.

So whilst the more skilful African players will continue to be picked off by European clubs, it seems unlikely that any one African side is ready to dominate the world. Maybe if they pool their resources and FIFA have the foresight to award the continent with the World Cup Final, things will change for the better and quicker.

Pele will probably never lift a World Cup . . . but his son may.

EURO
'92
FINALS

12-PAGE

SPECIAL

SECTION

Red and white . . .
DYNAMITE!

By GERRY COX

'WE are red, we are white, we are Danish dynamite,' sang Denmark's colourful fans as they watched their team blow up the hopes of the favourites and win the 1992 European Championship.

Denmark, 16–1 outsiders before the tournament began and 80–1 after they lost to Sweden, beat France, Holland and Germany, the three leading candidates, to become European champions. What is more, the great Danes did it in the style that once brought adulation from around the world for the brilliant Brazilians.

Like the unforgettable teams of Pelé, Vava and Garrincha, the Danes played with a type of joy and freedom not normally seen in the tense world of international football. Brilliant individuals and their skilful supporting team members played together in such an exhilarating way that they put a smile back on the face of football.

It was not just a victory for Danish coach Richard Moeller Nielsen and his previously little-known squad. It was a win for football and for underdogs everywhere. Skill had triumphed over the system.

A tournament that had been remarkable only for its dullness up to the semi-finals suddenly exploded into life when the Danes beat reigning champions Holland. And it climaxed with one of the most memorable finals in international football when the bruised and battered Danish footsoldiers overcame the mighty German stormtroopers to lift the Henri Delauney Trophy.

From the land of Hans Christian Andersen came one of international football's greatest fairytales. Denmark did not even know they would be taking part in Euro '92 until eight days before the finals began.

They had finished behind Yugoslavia in their qualifying group, as a series

OPPOSITE The greatest moment of Peter Schmeichel's football career as the brilliant Danish goalkeeper raises the Henri Delauney Trophy for all Europe to see.
(● *Read all about Peter the Great Dane and his Manchester fans on Page 100*).

of personal battles and a rebuilding process affected the team's results. But when the Yugoslavs were expelled from Sweden because of United Nations sanctions against their war-torn country, Denmark were invited to replace them.

But this, said the experts, was surely not the Denmark that had been so feared and respected in the 1980s. That team of international stars such as Morten Olsen, Michael Laudrup and Preber Elkjaer reached the European Championship semi-finals in 1984 and were fancied to win the 1986 World Cup before they committed footballing suicide against Spain.

The Class of '92, however, was considered ordinary by comparison. With Michael Laudrup and Liverpool's Jan Molby missing because of their disagreements with the coach, Denmark's biggest star was goalkeeper Peter Schmeichel, already a national hero.

Laudrup's younger brother Brian was also making a name for himself, with Bayern Munich in Germany, but he too had fallen out with Moeller Nielsen and had missed much of the past season because of injury. The rest of the squad were thought to be no more than honest journeymen, typical Danish players who earn their livings abroad.

Full-back John Sivebaek had left Manchester United for Monaco of France, captain Lars Olsen played in Turkey for Trabzonspor and striker Flemming Povlsen followed his club experience in Spain by joining Borussia Dortmund in Germany.

Also in the Bundesliga were forwards Bent Christensen and defender Henrik Andersen, but the rest of the squad played club football in Denmark. Striker Lars Elstrup returned to OB Odense from Luton Town and defender Kent Nielsen left Aston Villa for Aarhus.

The inexperience of the squad, coupled with their lack of preparation, meant that they were given little chance of winning in Sweden, and Kent Nielsen admitted: 'We all expected to play three group games and go home. No-one expected to reach even the semi-final.'

GROUP ONE contained host nation Sweden and England and France, joint third favourites to win the tournament. Here surely were to be found the stars of the tournament . . . England's captain Gary Lineker, in his final international tournament before retiring and searching the one goal he needed to equal Bobby Charlton's record of 49 England goals; Jean-Pierre Papin of France, European Footballer of the Year in his last season for Marseille before joining AC Milan in a multi-million pound deal—he was captain of Michel Platini's French team that had lost only twice in three years; Tomas Brolin, the young Swedish superstar who had set Italy alight with his midfield displays for Parma and promised to do the same for the host country.

GROUP TWO was even stronger. World champions Germany and reigning champions Holland were expected to cruise through to the semi-finals, with the CIS considered less of a threat than they had been when they were the Soviet Union. Scotland, it was assumed, were simply making up the numbers and would do well to avoid losing by cricket scores in all three games.

How wrong the experts were! While England and France failed to reach the semi-finals, Germany qualified only because Scotland thrashed the CIS 3–0, after threatening to do the same to the Germans. Indeed, if the Scots had possessed a finisher of the quality of Papin or Lineker, they would surely have humiliated the Germans in Norrkoping. But chances went begging while the German forwards capitalised on theirs to win 2–0.

That match, the second of Group Two, was the first to bring any excitement to the tournament. The whole structure of the finals was questioned after four of the opening five games produced tedious, tactical draws.

Sweden and France kicked off with a 1–1 draw in Stockholm, with the Swedes taking a surprise lead through defender Jan Eriksson's header before Papin equalised for France with an opportunist strike.

Denmark's first game was against England in Malmo, and for almost half an hour their lack of preparation was obvious. Nielsen said: 'No-one knew

Woodwork and Woods to the rescue

WHAT a difference two inches would have made! Stuart Pearce's free-kick hits the French crossbar. At the other end, Chris Woods (below) punches clear of the leaping Laurent Blanc.

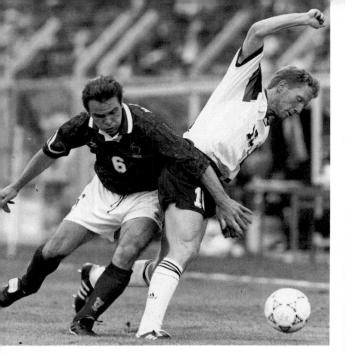

SCOTLAND may have lost two out of three but their courage won the cheers of the Swedish crowds. Here, fighting losing battles, are Brian McClair against Mathias Sammer (Germany) and on the right Stuart McCall in a determined tussle with Ruud Gullit (Holland).

★ ★

how close we came to blowing it in that first half-hour.' But survive they did, and could even have sneaked a win if Jensen's shot had not rebounded from the inside of the goalpost late in the game.

In Group Two, Holland finally produced a win, over Scotland, but looked below their best. Germany and the CIS eked out a poor 1–1 draw, with both sides struggling to find their rhythm.

The second round of matches was little better. This time Holland and CIS cancelled out each other in a goalless draw and it was the Germans who struggled to beat Scotland. In Group One, England and France played cat and mouse in a tedious 0–0 draw which was considered satisfactory by both managers. The public and media did not agree.

In Stockholm, Sweden went top of the group by beating Denmark 1–0 with a goal from Tomas Brolin, who was starting to impress. However, the Danes played well enough to have won and Schmeichel said: 'That gave us the belief in ourselves that we needed.'

The final games of each group were played simultaneously. Denmark, bottom of Group One, needed to beat France to qualify for the semi-finals. In the first

ANDY'S BONNIE BATTLERS

THEY'VE failed to qualify for the semi-finals, but Scotland and manager Andy Roxburgh (crouching) could not be happier after trouncing CIS 3–0.

★ ★

shock of the tournament, the Danes won 2–1 with goals from Henrik Larsen and Lars Elstrup too much for Papin's goal for France.

If England beat Sweden, they would at least go into the draw for the semi-finals. But after leading 1–0 through David Platt's third-minute goal, England were humiliated by a battling display from the Swedes, who could have won by more than 2–1 with another goal from Eriksson and a brilliant effort from Brolin.

So England and France were out and unfashionable Sweden and Denmark were through. There were no such upsets in Group Two, but the results were still surprising. Holland finally came good with a breathtaking 3–1 win over Germany in what many experts saw as a rehearsal of the final.

Meanwhile, the Scots surprised everyone and ensured a heroes' return with a superb 3–0 win over the CIS, as richly-deserved as any victory in the tournament. Andy Roxburgh's men may have gone out at the same stage as England, but they left Sweden with more pride and respect than Graham Taylor's shocked troops.

The England manager had told the people back home to 'sit back, put your

GETTING to grips with Basile Boli is Gary Lineker, but the French defender managed to stem another abortive England raid.

GOING FOR GRABS!

GETTING to grips in the same goalless encounter, David Platt could well be helping himself to the shirt of Frenchman Didier Deschamps as a souvenir before the final whistle.

★ ★

BALLET TIME

MOVEMENTS more in keeping with Covent Garden are demonstrated by David Batty and Sweden's Jonas Thern (below) and Martin Keown and Jean-Pierre Papin (France) on the right.

feet up in front of the television and enjoy us winning.' Instead, with the exception of a lively first half against Sweden, Taylor's baffling tactics and strange team selections meant that England finished bottom of the group without a win and with only one goal.

Even worse, Taylor had to endure massive public criticism for his decision to substitute Lineker half an hour from the end of the Sweden game, with England desperate for a goal. Not only was it tactical suicide, but it was seen as a public humiliation for one of football's finest servants.

It was a sad end to a great career, and there was further embarrassment for the English when hooligans went on the rampage in Stockholm after two nights of trouble in Malmo. With the exception of the Germans, no other fans caused major problems in a generally peaceful tournament. The Danes and the Swedes were the happiest fans, delighted to be through to the semi-finals.

Sweden had to play Germany, but were confident in front of their enthusiastic fans in Stockholm. They had an early setback, however, when Thomas Hassler scored with a curling free-kick over the Swedish defensive wall. It was the second time that Hassler had scored in such style, having earned the Germans a draw in the last minute against the CIS.

What Brolin did for Sweden, Hassler did even better for Germany. Fast-emerging as the player of the tournament so far, the little midfielder popped up all over the pitch to cause problems for Sweden.

After 58 minutes, Karlheinz Riedle made it 2–0 to Germany when he took advantage of terrible marking in the Swedish defence. Brolin pulled a goal back from the penalty spot soon afterwards but another goal from Riedle eased German nerves two minutes from time. Even then, the Swedes were not finished as Kennet Andersson scored with a header a minute later. Germany held on to win 3–2, but again were far from convincing.

In the other semi-final, in Gothenburg the following day, the Danes were thought to be out of their depth against the likes of Gullit, Van Basten, Rijkaard and Koeman, Holland's quartet of world-class stars. But on the first of two memorable evenings in the Ullevi Stadium, Denmark outplayed the Dutch at their own game and set the tournament alight.

With Laudrup and Povlsen striking fear into the Dutch defence, Denmark went ahead when Larsen scored with a header after five minutes. The Danes were playing the neater and more incisive football, weaving passes together and making the Dutch look clumsy.

However, Holland equalised midway through the first half when Dennis Bergkamp scored his third goal of the tournament with a shot from the edge of the area that deceived the previously faultless Schmeichel.

But Larsen, who had only just established himself in the starting line-up, scored his second goal with a thundering drive after 32 minutes. Denmark fully deserved their lead for the speed and fluency of their attacks and the way they blunted the Dutch masters. Rijkaard, Koeman and Jan Wouters were forced to resort to foul after foul as Laudrup and Jensen ran rings around them in midfield.

JOINT top scorer for the tournament with three goals was Karlheinz Riedle, but the German striker failed to find the target in the 3–1 defeat by Holland at Gothenburg.

JOYFUL moment for Tomas Brolin after the Swedish hot-shot had scored to seal England's fate in the Championship.

One kick too many led to Laudrup's substitution after an hour, and with him went Denmark's mastery. The Dutch began to take control, and an equaliser looked possible long before Rijkaard provided it in the closing minutes.

With the powerful Germans to be faced in the final, neither side wanted the added strain of extra time. Andersen had already been taken off on a stretcher, his kneecap broken by a collision with Van Basten. With so many walking wounded, Denmark hung on desperately for a penalty shoot-out.

When it arrived, Danish nerves held stronger than the Dutch. The Danes scored with all five penalties but Van Basten, of all people, had his shot saved by Schmeichel.

Denmark were through to the final and, even if their weary players were not to beat Germany, they had already done themselves proud. The build-up for the final, four days later, concentrated on Danish efforts to get their injured men fit. Laudrup, Sivebaek, Jensen, Olsen and Larsen were the main worries, while the Germans had no such problems. But come the final in Gothenburg, the Danes were not only fit but raring to go and beat the Germans.

The opening minutes suggested a change of strategy from Moeller Nielsen. Instead of the swift attacking and quick-passing game employed against Holland, the Danes were pacing themselves with slow, patient moves. Hassler versus Laudrup was billed as the match within a match to decide which of them would be voted Player of the Tournament. Initially Hassler was ahead, but Laudrup was destined to get the award and, a few days later, he moved to Fiorentina for a fee of £3.5 million.

Germany could have been two goals in front in the first 15 minutes but they found Schmeichel in commanding form. The big keeper blocked a Stefan Reuter shot from close range and tipped away a Klinsmann shot on the turn. Then, in the 18th minute, the Ullevi Stadium erupted into a sea of red and white.

German captain Andy Brehme was tackled in the left-back position and eventually Povlsen fed the ball from the right. Jensen, who had not scored for five years for Denmark, hit an unstoppable shot into the far corner of the net. Arsenal, his new club for £1.1 million, will hope for goals more frequently.

Still Germany went forward, but the Danish defence held strong. Frustration was evident as five German players and a Dane were booked for fouls. Then came two moments that sealed Denmark's win.

After 73 minutes, Jurgen Klinsmann sent a powerful header towards the roof of the net from close range, only for Schmeichel to produce a stunning save, tipping the ball over the bar. Five minutes later, Kim Vilfort wriggled through on the right of the penalty area. His shot hit the inside of the post before going into the net, and the Danes went wild.

It was an emotional moment for Vilfort, who had missed the game against France to return to Denmark, where his six-year-old daughter was awaiting a bone-marrow transplant in a bid to cure her of leukaemia. Vilfort had only returned to Sweden when his daughter and her younger brother asked why

'Here was proof that fairytales can still happen'

DENMARK know they have pulled off the 'impossible' after their second goal in the final with Germany—and scorer Kim Vilfort lies buried beneath this heap of happiness.

their father wasn't playing for his country. No-one deserved higher praise than the Brondby midfielder.

Here was proof that, in the sometimes cynical world of professional football, fairytales can still happen. And it was fitting that Pelé, Franz Beckenbauer and Bobby Charlton, three of world football's greatest names, were all present at that marvellous final in Gothenburg.

A tournament that had started in a muddle of dull, tactical draws had finished in thrilling style, with a heartwarming story and the outcome wanted by everyone who believes in football as the beautiful game.

FAREWELL sadly to the international scene for Gary Lineker. The England skipper was substituted in the 61st minute of their third disastrous group match against their Swedish hosts (● *IFB's tribute to Lineker on his departure to Japan starts on Page 72*).

Complete round-up of the 199

GROUP ONE

JUNE 10—Stockholm
Sweden 1 (Eriksson 24)
France 1 (Papin 59)
HT: 1–0. **Att**: 29,860. **Ref**: Spirin (CIS)
Sweden: Ravelli—R. Nilsson, J. Eriksson, P. Andersson, Björklund—Ingesson, Schwarz, Thern, Limpar—K. Andersson (Dahlin 74), Brolin.
France: Martini—Boli, Blanc, Casoni—Angloma (Fernandez 65), Cantona, Sauzee, Deschamps, Amoros—Papin, Vahirua (Perez 46).

JUNE 11—Malmö
Denmark 0
England 0
Att: 26,385. **Ref**: Blankenstein (Hol)
Denmark: Schmeichel—K. Nielsen, Olsen, Christofte—Sivebaek, Vilfort, Jensen, Laudrup, Andersen—B. Christensen, Povlsen.
England: Woods—Curle (Daley 61), Keown, Walker, Pearce—Palmer, Steven, Platt, Merson (Webb 70)—Lineker, Smith.

JUNE 14—Malmö
France 0
England 0
Att: 26,535. **Ref**: Puhl (Hun)
France: Martini—Boli, Blanc, Casoni—Amoros, Sauzee (Angloma 46), Fernandez (Perez 75), Durrand, Deschamps—Cantona, Papin.
England: Woods—Palmer, Keown, Walker, Pearce—Sinton, Steven, Platt, Batty—Lineker, Shearer.

JUNE 14—Stockholm
Sweden 1 (Brolin 59)
Denmark 0
HT: 0–0. **Att**: 29,902. **Ref**: Schmidhuber (Ger)
Sweden: Ravelli—R. Nilsson, J. Eriksson, P. Andersson, Björklund—Ingesson, Schwarz, Thern, Limpar (Erlingmark 89)—Dahlin (Ekström 76), Brolin.
Denmark: Schmeichel—K. Nielsen, Olsen, Christofte—Sivebaek, Vilfort, Jensen (Larsen 62), Andersen—Laudrup—Povlsen, B. Christensen (Frank 51).

JUNE 17—Stockholm
Sweden 2 (Eriksson 51, Brolin 82)
England 1 (Platt 3)
HT: 0–1. **Att**: 30,126. **Ref**: Rosa dos Santos (Por)
Sweden: Ravelli—R. Nilsson, J. Eriksson, P. Andersson, Björklund—Ingesson, Schwarz, Thern, Limpar (Ekström 46)—Dahlin, Brolin.

England: Woods—Batty, Keown, Walker, Pearce—Daley, Palmer, Webb, Sinton (Merson 76)—Lineker (Smith 61), Platt.

JUNE 17—Malmö
France 1 (Papin 61)
Denmark 2 (Larsen 7, Elstrup 78)
HT: 0–1. **Att**: 25,673. **Ref**: Forstinger (Aus)
France: Martini—Boli, Blanc, Casoni—Amoros, Deschamps, Perez (Cocard 80), Durand—Cantona, Papin, Vahirua (Fernandez 46).
Denmark: Schmeichel—K. Nielsen (Piechnik 62), Olsen, Christofte—Sivebaek, Larsen, Jensen, Andersen—Laudrup (Elstrup 69)—Povlsen, Frank.

Table	P	W	D	L	F	A	Pts
SWEDEN	3	2	1	0	4	2	5
DENMARK	3	1	1	1	2	2	3
France	3	0	2	1	2	3	2
England	3	0	2	1	1	2	2

GROUP TWO

JUNE 12—Norrköping
CIS 1 (Dobrovolski 62 pen)
Germany 1 (Hässler 89)
HT: 0–0. **Att**: 17,410. **Ref**: Biguet (Fr)
CIS: Kharin—O. Kuznetsov, Chernishov, Tsveiba—Kanchelskis, Mikhailichenko, Liuti (Onopko 46), Kolivanov, D. Kuznetsov, Shalimov (Ivanov 81)—Dobrovolski.
Germany: Illgner—Binz—Reuter (Klinsmann 63), Kohler, Buchwald, Brehme—Hässler, Effenberg, Doll—Voller (Möller 46), Riedle.

JUNE 12—Gothenburg
Holland 1 (Bergkamp 77)
Scotland 0
HT: 0–0. **Att**: 35,720. **Ref**: Karlsson (Swe)
Holland: Van Breukelen—Van Aerle, Koeman, Van Tiggelen—Rijkaard, Wouters (Jonk 55), Witschge—Gullit, Bergkamp (Winter 85), Roy—Van Basten.
Scotland: Goram—McKimmie, Gough, McPherson, Malpas—McAllister, McStay, McCall, McClair (Ferguson 79)—Durie, McCoist (Gallacher 75).

JUNE 15—Norrköping
Scotland 0
Germany 2 (Riedle 29, Effenberg 46).
HT: 0–1. **Att**: 16,638. **Ref**: Goethals (Bel)
Scotland: Goram—McKimmie, Gough, McPherson, Malpas—McAllister, McStay, McCall, McClair—Durie (Nevin 55), McCoist (Gallacher 70).
Germany: Illgner—Kohler, Binz, Buchwald—Hässler, Effenberg, Möller, Sammer, Brehme—Klinsmann, Riedle (Reuter 69, Schulz 74).

uropean Championship finals

JUNE 15—Gothenburg
Holland 0
CIS 0
Att: 34,440. **Ref**: Mikelsen (Den)
Holland: Van Breukelen—Van Aerle, Koeman, Van Tiggelen—Rijkaard, Wouters, Witschge—Gullit (Van't Schip 71), Bergkamp (Viscaal 80), Roy—Van Basten.
CIS: Kharin — Chernishov — O. Kuznetsov — Kanchelskis, Tsveiba, Onopko—Mikhailichenko, Dobrovolski, Kolivanov, Aleinikov (D. Kuznetsov 57)—Yuran (Kiriakov 66).

JUNE 18—Gothenburg
Holland 3 (Rijkaard 2, Witschge 14, Bergkamp 71)
Germany 1 (Klinsmann 53)
HT: 2–0. **Att**: 37,725. **Ref**: Pairetto (Italy)
Holland: Van Breukelen—Van Tiggelen, Koeman, De Boer (Winter 61)—Rijkaard, Wouters, Witschge—Gullit, Bergkamp (Bosz 87), Roy—Van Basten
Germany: Illgner—Binz (Sammer 46)—Brehme, Kohler, Frontzeck—Hässler, Effenberg, Helmer, Möller—Klinsmann, Riedle (Doll 76).

JUNE 18—Norrköping
Scotland 3 (McStay 6, McClair 17, McAllister 84 pen)
CIS 0
HT: 2–0. **Att**: 14,600. **Ref**: Röthlisberger (Swz)
Scotland: Goram—McKimmie, Gough, McPherson, Boyd—McAllister, McStay, McClair, McCall—Gallacher (Nevin 79), McCoist (McInally 67).
CIS: Kharin—O. Kuznetsov, Chernishov, Tchadadze—Kanchelskis, Mikhailichenko, Dobrovolski, Aleinikov (D. Kuznetsov 46), Onopko—Kiriakov (Korneyev 46), Yuran.

Table	P	W	D	L	F	A	Pts
HOLLAND	3	2	1	0	4	1	5
GERMANY	3	1	1	1	4	4	3
Scotland	3	1	0	2	3	3	2
CIS	3	0	2	1	1	4	2

SEMI-FINALS

JUNE 21—Stockholm
Sweden 2 (Brolin 64 pen, K. Andersson 89)
Germany 3 (Hässler 10, Riedle 58, 88)
HT: 0–1. **Att**: 28,827. **Ref**: Lanese (Italy)
Sweden: Ravelli—R. Nilsson, J. Eriksson, Björklund, Ljung—K. Andersson, Ingesson, Thern, J. Nilsson (Limpar 59)—Dahlin (Ekström 72), Brolin.
Germany: Illgner—Reuter, Kohler, Helmer, Buchwald, Brehme—Hässler, Effenberg, Sammer—Klinsmann (Doll 89), Riedle.

JUNE 22—Gothenburg
Holland 2 (Bergkamp 23, Rijkaard 85)
Denmark 2 (Larsen 5, 32)
HT: 1–2. **90 min.**: 2–2. **Att**: 37,450. **Ref**: Soriano Aladren (Sp)
Denmark 5–4 on penalties:
Shoot-out sequence (Holland first): Koeman 1–0, Larsen 1–1; Van Basten saved, Povlsen 1–2; Bergkamp 2–2, Elstrup 2–3; Rijkaard 3–3, Vilfort 3–4; Witschge 4–4, Christofte 4–5.
Holland: Van Breukelen—Van Tiggelen, R. Koeman, De Boer (Kieft 46)—Rijkaard, Wouters, Witschge—Gullit, Bergkamp, Roy (Van't Schip 115)—Van Basten.
Denmark: Schmeichel—Piechnik, L. Olsen, Christofte—Sivebaek, Vilfort, Jensen, Larsen, Andersen (Claus Christensen 68)—Povlsen, Laudrup (Elstrup 57).

FINAL

JUNE 26—Gothenburg
Germany 0
Denmark 2 (Jensen 18, Vilfort 78)
HT: 0–1. **Att**: 37,800. **Ref**: Galler (Swz)
Germany: Illgner—Reuter, Kohler, Helmer, Buchwald, Brehme—Hässler, Effenberg (Thom 80), Sammer (Doll 45)—Klinsmann, Riedle.
Denmark: Schmeichel—Piechnik, Olsen, K. Nielsen—Sivebaek (Christiansen 66), Vilfort, Jensen, Larsen, Christofte—Povlsen, Laudrup.

GOALSCORERS

THREE: Bergkamp (Hol), Brolin (Swe), Larsen (Swe), Riedle (Ger).
TWO: Eriksson (Swe), Hässler (Ger), Papin (Fr), Rijkaard (Hol).
ONE: Dobrovolski (CIS), Elstrup, Jensen, Vilfort (Den), Effenberg, Klinsmann (Ger), McAllister, McClair, McStay (Sco), Platt (Eng), Witschge (Hol), K. Andersson (Swe).

HAIL the Prince of Denmark—the man voted Player of the Tournament—Brian Laudrup, now with Fiorentina in a £3·5 million deal with Bayern Munich completed shortly after the Championship final.

Sheffield's wise and not-so-old Owl flies high again

By DENNIS SIGNY (Sunday Express)

Trevor Francis still gets that wonderful feeling after scoring—in fact probably doubly so as a player-manager. Here he takes off after scoring Sheffield Wednesday's winner against Forest.

TREVOR Francis, one of the new breed of soccer managers with the financial clout to be able to be his own man, guided Sheffield Wednesday into Europe in his first season in charge at Hillsborough after the unexpected departure of Ron Atkinson to Aston Villa.

Wednesday, something of a yo-yo team over the years, had only gained promotion back to the First Division at the first attempt in 1991 in third place behind Oldham Athletic and West Ham United.

Under Francis, who had joined Wednesday as a player after a rocky managerial baptism at Queens Park Rangers, the side finished in an impressive third place behind champions Leeds United and Manchester United to ensure not only a place in the new Premier League but a crack at European football in the UEFA Cup. This was quite a feat for the former England international, who celebrated his 38th birthday on the Easter Sunday as the championship race drew to a close. It had been thirty years since Wednesday, champions of the First Division in 1903, 1904, 1929 and 1930, had finished so high. They were runners-up in 1961.

Europe, too, was an unexpected bonus. Wednesday were twice in the old Fairs Cup in the Sixties, the last time in 1964, but although they won the Rumbelows League Cup under Atkinson in 1991, only one English team was allowed into Europe at that time.

Atkinson might have sown the seeds for success before his unexpected and controversial departure to Villa Park in June 1991, but it is fair to say that not even the most diehard supporter of the Owls would have contemplated in his wildest dreams what would happen under Francis. Wednesday played some of the best football in the league.

The extrovert Atkinson was a hard act to follow. And Francis, whose reign at QPR as successor to Jim Smith was littered with headlines of the wrong sort, admitted that his directive at the start of the season was to ensure that Wednesday maintained their position in the league to be involved in the new Premier Division. Consolidation following promotion was the aim—yet Oldham, who had gone up as champions six points ahead of the Owls, struggled and West Ham, the runners-up, were relegated.

Francis, looking back on the season, was reluctant to single out an individual for the club's success though any manager would be pleased about the likes of David Hirst, whose goals made a great contribution. Hirst, who was given an international blooding by England manager Graham Taylor, proved a prolific marksman. He missed out on selection for the European Championship in Sweden but is clearly still a goalscorer for the future as England look to replace Gary Lineker.

Chris Woods was established as England's number one goalkeeper and, despite having thirteen goals against him in heavy defeats by Leeds and Arsenal, gained the confidence of the Hillsborough faithful with a series of clean sheets.

Carlton Palmer, who became Wednesday's record signing when Atkinson paid West Bromwich Albion £750,000 for him in February 1989, benefited from Wednesday's success and was drafted into the England set-up by Taylor, ultimately earning a place in the European Championship squad.

Roland Nilsson, Wednesday's £375,000 signing from IFK Gothenburg, scored his first goal for the Hillsborough club in eighty-six games during the season. He, too, went to the European Championship to play for Sweden.

Although John Sheridan proved reluctant to agree a new contract with Wednesday at the end of the season, Francis was happy to pay tribute to the role over the year of the Republic of Ireland midfielder, who had scored the winning goal against Manchester United in the previous season's Rumbelows Cup Final.

So, despite the traumas caused by Atkinson's departure, the Owls flew high. Europe might have been an unexpected bonus, an adventure for players and supporters, but it was a return to familiar pastures for the manager. Francis scored the European Cup Final winner for Nottingham Forest in 1979 against Malmo and apart from winning fifty-two caps for England and playing on many foreign fields, he enjoyed success with Sampdoria and Atalanta in Italy.

The Plymouth-born superstar, who was Britain's first £1 million player when he joined Forest from Birmingham City in February 1979, certainly erased the unhappy memories of his managerial period at QPR in his first year in charge of Wednesday.

If ever a manager learned the hard way from his mistakes it was Francis. During his eleven turbulent months in charge at QPR, he upset players by

The unexpected departure of Ron Atkinson (above) from the manager's office at Hillsborough gave Trevor Francis a second chance to prove himself as the boss.

trying to change their eating and training habits. He criticised them in public and his decision to fine Martin Allen two weeks' wages for leaving the squad at Newcastle to attend the birth of his son was raised in the House of Commons.

He described his players as 'greedy and disloyal' in a tabloid newspaper article, he was reported to the Professional Footballers Association and one player even spoke about being substituted in a reserve game because he had criticised Francis for making a bad pass.

Given a second chance by Wednesday, Francis said: 'I don't want to dwell on the past. We all make mistakes and we should all learn from them.' He proved he had. He was more aware of his public statements, but his standard of discipline and the importance of attacking football remained the same.

Atkinson, who took Francis to Hillsborough as a player, was obviously an influence on him. Francis was a shrewd dealer in the transfer market. The £350,000 he paid for Leyton Orient teenager Chris Bart-Williams looks to be a bargain.

Yet Francis proved with the Owls that he was still prepared to grab the nettles. When Gordon Watson won a controversial penalty against Leeds in a televised game, Francis spoke out in strong terms. 'I have had a word or two with Gordon Watson and he knows my feelings,' he said. 'I am pleased to earn penalties, but I am not happy to have gained one in circumstances like that. The player was wrong.'

Francis called for referees to book 'play-acting' players—as is done in Italy.

Brian Clough once called Francis 'too nice'. At QPR he became 'Britain's most hated manager'. Yet, as one critic observed, Hillsborough seemed to suit Francis as much as Loftus Road disagreed with him. He found the sort of rapport with the Yorkshire supporters that he enjoyed at Birmingham in his prodigy days as a player, yet he insists that his style of man-management is the same as it was in those unhappy days at QPR.

However you analyse it, the Owls under Trevor Francis are flying high.

Jim Smith, known evermore as 'Bald Eagle', was a hard act for Trevor to follow on his baptism as a manager at QPR through eleven turbulent months.

South America

SPIRIT OF '70

These were great days for Brazil and Pele, seen here celebrating after the 4–1 defeat of Italy in the 1970 World Cup Final in Mexico.

AND IN '94?

Now Brazil are hoping to emulate Pele's men 24 years later in USA. There were clear signs of a reawakening at Wembley in 1992 in the 1–1 draw with England. Here Luiz Henrique outpaces Des Walker.

up and running

Twin giants are back with gold in mind

ARGENTINA are building on their South American championship triumph and Brazil have emerged from an uninspiring period of their rich football history. The South American challenge for the 1994 World Cup is up and running, with its two giants at the front of the field.

It would seem the chances of the trophy returning to South America are fifty-fifty considering Brazil, Argentina and Uruguay have accounted for exactly half of the winners in the fourteen previous competitions.

Although Italy and Germany have won the World Cup as many times as Brazil, it is the three winning teams in gold shirts possessing breathtaking players that stay in the memory.

The ultimate exponents of skilful football were the Brazilian team that dominated the 1970 World Cup in Mexico. Gerson, Jairzinho, Tostao and, of course, Pele captured the World's imagination when they finished the tournament by thrashing Italy 4–1.

Coach Carlos Alberto Parreira was a minor figure in the 1970 set-up, but twenty years later he was thrust into the thick of the action. Faced with the task of hauling Brazilian football out of the doldrums, Parreira set about the task in admirable style, with 1970 manager Mario Zagala as his technical co-ordinator.

After being appointed head coach in 1991 Parreira, who never played football professionally, immediately advocated a return to the attractive football that became synonymous with Brazil. Results were important but encouraging and developing a player's 'love affair with the ball' was to be of paramount importance.

Rather than reduce Brazil's potency, Parreira's traditional methods rejuvenated the national team. This was not easy, as morale could not have been lower before Parreira took over. The football-loving nation, already

SPECIAL REPORT by LEE WELLINGS

staying away from top domestic games because of increasing hooliganism, had become disillusioned with their country's poor performances.

Brazilian teams of the late eighties sacrificed some of the natural flair and sought wins above all else. Results were poor and a cynical element crept into their play. This became a serious problem for them in their disastrous South American Championship campaign of 1991.

Falcao, who made a name for himself in the 1982 World Cup, had progressed to manager, but his heavily-criticised team stumbled into the final stages with an eighty-ninth minute goal against Ecuador.

Five players were sent off in an explosive match against Argentina, three of them Brazilians, and wins against Colombia and Chile could not save Falcao from the sack. Former managers, like Tele Santana, were queuing up to mourn publicly the state of Brazilian football, but many players survived this era to flourish under Parreira. Luiz Henrique, Neto and Rai ran defences ragged in friendlies, Branco's left foot looked better with every ferocious free-kick, and striker Bebeto came of age.

Bebeto, the highest-paid footballer in Brazil, was given the nickname 'Chorao', meaning cry-baby, when his impetuous streak became noticeable. For instance, he deserted the squad for the South American Championship when told he was left out for their opening match. But under Perreira, he is accumulating caps and goals and showing the form that made him one of the best strikers in the world.

All of Bebeto's proposed transfers to Europe fell through, but the stars who did make it to Italy are invaluable to Brazil. Players like top striker Careca, first-choice goalkeeper Taffarel and the gifted midfielder Dunga are often unavailable for friendlies because of Italian duties, but Brazilian managers have learned how to adjust to this problem and to be patient.

Another problem faced by Parreira and his predecessors is the Brazilian press and their crusades. When they continually stated that Junior, an ageing hero, should be brought back into the side, Parreira kept them happy by using him — as a substitute.

There will surely be other stumbling blocks on the way to the 1994 World Cup finals, but if and when Brazil qualify, they will want to avoid the biggest obstacle of all, Argentina. As well as beating Brazil to the South American Championship, Argentina have managed to stay a step ahead of their fiercest rivals in recent World Cup competitions.

In 1982 they helped block Brazil's passage to the semi-finals. In 1990 Claudio Caniggia's goal sent Brazil home. And Argentina have won the tournament twice, in 1978 and 1986, since Brazil last came out on top.

Argentina have confounded the people who dubbed them 'a one-man team' when Diego Maradona ruled. Although many of their achievements have to be attributed to Maradona, they are coping perfectly well without him.

When Carlos Bilardo resigned after taking Argentina to the 1990 World Cup Final, Alfio 'Coco' Basile was appointed as national team coach. There was an element of surprise in the choice of Basile, a defender/midfielder with Racing

'Showing the form that made him one of the best strikers in the world'

A fine action study of Bebeto, the highest-paid footballer in Brazil, now rapidly collecting caps and goals after a problematic start to his international career.

Club in the 1960s; previous managers such as Carlos Bilardo and Cesar Menotti had managed a leading club before taking on the national job.

The relatively-inexperienced Basile relished the challenge, though, and started on a good note by improving the country's tarnished image. Argentina had developed a reputation for ill discipline, culminating in disgraceful scenes of fouling, cheating and swearing in the 1990 World Cup Final.

Although they were no angels during the South American Championships in Chile, the new faces introduced by Basile shifted the emphasis to positive football. They were rewarded with the trophy.

Argentina are using creative, attacking midfielders such as Diego Simeone and Dario Franco to supplement their strikers. Diego Latorre is regarded by many as the best of the bunch of midfielders able to score valuable goals for Argentina. He made his debut against Hungary early in 1991 and, soon afterwards, his performances for Boca Juniors and Argentina prompted the Italian club Fiorentina to sign him. They also bought another key Argentinian player at the same time in striker Gabriel Batistuta. He has been a sensation for club and country and should enjoy many more years of international football.

Basile's use of young talent suggests a rosy future for Argentina, but other South American nations have good reason to expect a bright future.

Colombia and Paraguay's under-23 players surprisingly qualified to represent South America at the Barcelona Olympics at the expense of Brazil and Argentina. And the full international sides these countries put out are capable of beating the best.

Colombia in particular are renowned for neat, incisive football which pleases the crowds but is not always as penetrative as it should be. If they qualify for the World Cup in USA, they certainly have the characters to enliven the competition, as they did in Italia '90 when they reached the second stage before losing to two goals by Cameroon's Roger Milla.

One is Rene Higuita, the eccentric goalkeeper whose mad dashes from his penalty area can be inspired or suicidal; indeed, Milla benefitted from Higuita's most infamous excursion. After a spell in Spain, Higuita has returned to Colombian football, where he is a hero.

Carlos Valderrama, the Colombian captain with skills as outrageous as his haircut, has also returned home from Europe. He never produced his best form in France and Spain but rarely lets Colombia down.

Colombia's problem is that they are in Argentina's group with only one team qualifying automatically—the runners-up face a play-off. Dark horses Paraguay and Peru make up a strong four-team group.

Uruguay, World Cup winners in 1930 and 1950, are advantageously placed in Group B with Brazil and are favourites to qualify above Ecuador, Bolivia and Venezuela.

As for Chile, previous bad behaviour means they are suspended from the 1994 World Cup. Ironically, they have put together a decent side, but it is still a class below the South American countries with a good chance of winning in 1994—Brazil and Argentina.

I know I'm a funny voice here but that doesn't worry me

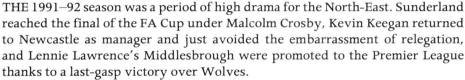

THE 1991–92 season was a period of high drama for the North-East. Sunderland reached the final of the FA Cup under Malcolm Crosby, Kevin Keegan returned to Newcastle as manager and just avoided the embarrassment of relegation, and Lennie Lawrence's Middlesbrough were promoted to the Premier League thanks to a last-gasp victory over Wolves.

In footballing circles, Lennie Lawrence is justifiably regarded as something of a miracle worker. Any man with the ability to keep Charlton in the First Division for five years, despite a shoestring budget and a myriad of unwelcome distractions, deserves such an epithet.

Following the 1991–92 season, Middlesbrough fans were entitled to agree.

By NICK GREEN

Andy Peyton was one of
Lawrence's important
signings, for a fee of £750,000
from Hull City.

By leading the North-East club to the lucrative profits of the Premier League
in his first season as manager, Lawrence earned the respect and adoration that
a man of his experience and ability warranted.

Almost as importantly for the fervent Boro fans, their team were established
as the North-East top dogs, a position which in no way surprised Lawrence.
'We are the best club, footballing and finance wise, in the North-East,' he
said, 'but the case will be that the other two (*Newcastle and Sunderland*) are
made bigger by the huge media hype towards them.'

Lawrence's success is fully deserved. Between 1982 and 1991 his sagacity
was reponsible for making Charlton a name in British football. The difficulty
he had in reaching the First Division was nothing compared to the difficulty
he had in keeping them there. Four times they appeared destined to slip into
the dogfight of the second division and four times they produced a late string
of results to avoid the drop. The name of Lennie Lawrence is, and always will
be, synonymous with escape.

He is convinced he is a better manager now. He has learned not to expect
too much. Any manager whose club has been through a winding-up order
in the High Court learns to appreciate the finer things in football that
Middlesbrough are able to provide.

But Lawrence still has a place in his heart for his old club. 'The whole system
was geared towards trying to get back to The Valley,' he said. 'In my last
days at Charlton even the team took second place to that obsession. Hopefully,
soon they will be able to concentrate on getting results.'

Even so, he realises that there can only be so much room for sentiment.
With Middlesbrough, Lawrence has the resources, the support and the players
to make success a real possibility.

'It was very difficult at Charlton,' he said, 'The gap between the big clubs
and the little clubs is getting larger and larger. Finance is all geared to the
big clubs and in that way I think the Premier League is motivated by greed.

'At Charlton I sold all my best players for a total of almost £4 million—and
I was not really allowed to re-invest much of that. What chance did I have?'

The people in the North-East have a reputation for being friendly and easy-
going. The avuncular, ebullient Lennie Lawrence is in his element in such an
environment. He has always had a superb Press, largely because of his honesty
and candour.

His temperament is his greatest attribute. As a southerner it could have
been difficult for him in such a different atmosphere, but he laughs at this
suggestion. 'I know very few people outside those at the club, but I am quite
happy with that. There must be no sentiment. We have a rule that players
must live within forty miles of the club and I must abide by this myself. I
know I am a funny voice here but it doesn't bother me. I have such a lot
of work to do.'

He relishes having the licence to run the club as he pleases. The ambiguity
of his role at Charlton, where his influence was anything but volitional, is
very much a thing of the past. At Middlesbrough he is given full opportunity

to prove his diligence and ability and to exercise the man-management in which he revels. Lawrence takes on a variety of jobs—eg, the technical side, the team organisation and the tactics—and he hates to be thought of as just a glorified coach.

In the first three months of his tenure, he released Tony Mowbray to Celtic for £1 million and Ian Baird for £350,000 to Hearts. He used this money to buy Andy Peyton from Hull City for £750,000, and Willie Falconer and Paul Wilkinson from Watford.

This proved to be inspired, for Wilkinson was the club's top scorer for the 1991–92 season with twenty-four goals. None was more important than the winner against Wolves in the last match of the season—the goal that automatically took them to the highest echelons and saved them from the purgatory of the play-offs.

Lawrence also led Middlesbrough to the semi-finals of the Rumbelows Cup in the same season, and it took a late goal in extra time from Manchester United's Ryan Giggs to deprive them of a trip to Wembley.

Lawrence is a man confident of his own ability and prudence. 'Boro will not lose money while I am manager, I can assure them of that,' he said. 'I have never been one for carte blanche irresponsibility.' Understatement of the year.

'This job needed someone with a working knowledge of the game who was different from the people they have had before,' he added. 'It would have

A hero returns to Newcastle! And here he is, Kevin Keegan, pictured on the touchline with his assistant Terry McDermott as United beat Bristol City 3–0.

been foolhardy for anyone inexperienced to have been appointed to this job.'

This brings us aptly on to the trials and tribulations of Newcastle United.

In February 1992, Sir John Hall, entrepreneur and club chairman, played his last card in appointing Kevin Keegan as manager in a bid to rejuvenate his youngsters' flagging limbs and restore parity with their North-East rivals. It was a curious change of heart from Keegan, who seven years earlier had said that he would never return from his life of luxury in Spain and become a football manager, whether the call came from Lancaster Gate, Anfield or the boys from the Gallowgate End. But in reality, the lure of a return to St. James Park proved too much and, amid hysterical scenes of jubilation at the return of the prodigal son, Keegan entered the world of management.

The sceptics said that it was a ridiculous appointment—Keegan had no experience in the field and would have no real idea how to advise a team languishing dangerously close to the bottom of the division. Surely, the symbiotic combination of the coaching and the administration would prove too difficult and he would only serve to exacerbate the problem.

Others countered that the team would be carried on a crest of a wave of optimism all the way to safety, under the most popular man in Newcastle since the days of 'Wor Jackie' Milburn.

The truth lay somewhere in between. Initially Keegan's boys were inspired and began to climb the table steadily, but after the euphoria had died down, a number of boardroom disputes and financial disagreements rocked the club back on its heels.

Keegan went walkabout and threatened to quit, complaining that he had not received the money he was promised to enter the transfer market, and

PROUD is the word for FA Cup Final managers of the day Ronnie Moran (Liverpool) and Malcolm Crosby (Sunderland).

Moments of pride

Newcastle United's survival was in doubt until the last game of the season. At least the denouement was satisfactory, although to many it appeared that the choice of manager was based on sentiment rather than logic.

The other big club in the North-East fared rather better in 1991–92. Not only was it the year that Sunderland achieved city status, and the year when the influx of Japanese industry threatened to lift the city out of the economic doldrums, but it was also The Year of the Cup Final!

Sunderland defeated West Ham, Chelsea and Norwich on the road to Wembley and although they found a revitalised Liverpool far too strong in the final, they could afford to hold their heads up high. The story was all the more remarkable because Denis Smith, Sunderland's manager for over four years, was sacked after Christmas '91, and the coach Malcolm Crosby prepared to walk out too, in a show of solidarity.

Smith persuaded Crosby to stay, and he was given the position of caretaker manager. When Sunderland defeated Norwich in the 1992 FA Cup semi-final, the directors realised their obligation to Crosby and gave him a one-year contract.

Leading the team out at Wembley was a dream come true for Crosby, a Sunderland fanatic all his life, and a supporter on the terraces the last time Sunderland were in the final, way back in 1973.

In the end—a season of oscillating fortunes for the North-East and the year of three men; the coming of Malcolm Crosby, the controversy of Kevin Keegan and, yet again, the talent of Lennie Lawrence, perhaps the most unheralded manager in the league.

. . . and joy

JOY was to follow ninety minutes later, but only for the victors Liverpool and Mark Wright, watched by Royalty and the Prime Minister.

Golden Oldies
. . . and still plenty of mileage left in their tanks

By HARRY PRATT

David O'Leary, signed for Arsenal as an apprentice, was still going strong at Highbury after 700 first-team appearances.

ONE of the lasting memories from the tense conclusion to the 1991–92 Barclays League season in England was the prominent part Gordon Strachan and Bryan Robson played for their respective teams, Leeds and Manchester United.

The former Old Trafford team-mates, both in their mid-thirties, suffered contrasting fortunes as the season reached its climax. While Strachan, the Leeds skipper, was present in all but one of Leeds' last seventeen matches, Robson was conspicuous by his absence in the Manchester United midfield.

What the two have proved, above all else, is that a player entering the twilight of his career can be just as effective as ever he was. This point is supported by the large number of experienced players, well into their thirties, who still command the same respect and attention from the opposition that they enjoyed in their earlier years.

When Howard Wilkinson, the Leeds manager, paid Manchester United £300,000 for Strachan in March 1989, he must have envisaged the influence the midfielder could have on his plans to build a side capable of challenging for the game's top honours.

Strachan, the 1991 Player of the Year, epitomises the dedicated football professional and it was fitting that he lifted the League Championship trophy in 1992, a reward for his tireless work, enthusiasm, gifted passing and astute footballing brain.

So impressive was he at Elland Road that Scotland manager Andy Roxburgh did not hesitate in recalling Strachan to the national squad. Unfortunately for Roxburgh, Strachan has been forced to retire from international football due to a long-term back injury which could also end his playing days at club level.

Meanwhile Robson remains, after a decade as captain at Old Trafford, the driving force of Manchester United. The former England captain has been plagued by serious injury throughout his career but this has done nothing to dampen his enthusiasm. The importance of Robson to United was never better illustrated than during their ill-fated 1991–92 League campaign.

When Robson played they seldom lost and usually won, but of the fifteen League games he missed, United achieved victory in only five. This failure to cope without Robson's stabilising influence eventually led to the title heading towards Yorkshire.

While these two captured the headlines in the 1991–92 English season, there were plenty of others testifying by their continuing excellence that there is life beyond thirty in the most demanding and frantic domestic league in the world.

Arsenal and Republic of Ireland central defender David O'Leary, currently the longest-serving player at Highbury, is still going strong more than fifteen years after signing for the club as an apprentice and, during the 1991–92 campaign, he made his 700th first-team appearance. Jack Charlton, the Eire manager, still considers that O'Leary's experience and composure are vital ingredients of his national team.

One of O'Leary's former Arsenal team-mates, defender Viv Anderson, continued to grace the Sheffield Wednesday team with his elegant style. As the former England international was approaching his thirty-sixth birthday, he was offered a new contract by the club—proof positive that he has lost none of his outstanding quality at the highest levels of the game.

Then there is Queens Park Rangers' captain, Ray Wilkins. Wilkins, a month younger than Anderson, is as potent as ever in midfield, extremely fit and, at present, it would seem there is no end in sight for the player capped eighty-four times by England between 1976 and 1987.

TOP LEFT Peter Reid enjoyed a first full season as player-manager at Manchester City. TOP RIGHT Cyrill Regis was an incredibly shrewd free signing by Ron Atkinson on Aston Villa's behalf.

International team-mate Andy Sinton says of his inspirational skipper: 'Ray is so fit that I see him playing at the top level until he is forty if he remains free of injury.'

Player-managers are now a developing feature in the English Premier Division. Ever since Kenny Dalglish proved at Liverpool that it is possible to combine the two jobs successfully, there has been a growing trend towards this type of appointment. That can only increase after further successes during the 1991–92 season.

Peter Reid, in his thirty-fifth year when he became manager of Manchester City in November 1990, enjoyed a good first full season at the helm. He has continued to add tenacity to City's midfield and has now been joined at the club by another player entering the final straight of his career, former Liverpool and England international Steve McMahon.

Then there is Sheffield Wednesday player-boss Trevor Francis. He uses himself sparingly these days, normally from the substitutes bench, but guiding Wednesday into third place behind the two Uniteds in the 1992 Championship and therefore booking a place in the UEFA Cup was a most creditable effort in his first season as Wednesday manager.

When Aston Villa manager Ron Atkinson acquired Cyrille Regis on a free transfer from Coventry in August 1991, many thought Regis, then thirty-three,

was past his best. But in the following season the striker justified Atkinson's faith by making no fewer than forty-three appearances and scoring ten times. He was one of the most consistent performers throughout his first season at Villa Park.

So, while it seems that players making their debuts in the Football League are getting younger every year, there is evidence that many of our top footballers will be speeding past that mythical 'thirty limit' in the new built-up areas of the Premier League.

And they've still plenty of mileage left in the tank!

Former England captain Bryan Robson has had his share of injuries but his enthusiasm for the game is as strong as ever.

THIRD TIME LUCKY

Klaus earns his place in German hall of fame

That's it at last! Werder Bremen skipper Klaus Allofs hoists the Cup Winners Cup high in triumph after a memorable match in Lisbon.

THE thirteen-year quest of Klaus Allofs for a European club football title finally ended in triumph when he led German side Werder Bremen to victory in the Cup Winners' Cup Final in 1992. At the age of thirty-five, the legendary German striker scored his side's first goal and made the second for New Zealand

Werder Bremen victory smiles—and now is the time for scrapbook pictures.

international Wynton Rufer in the 2–0 defeat of Monaco on a memorable night in Lisbon.

It was the crowning glory in a marvellous career for the experienced forward, who was a fixture in the West German national side for most of the 1980s. Only the hard-hearted could have begrudged him the glorious sense of achievement and fulfilment. It proved third time lucky for him in a European final and, not surprisingly, the spotlight focussed on the Old Man of German Football at the final whistle.

His seemingly eternal search for a winner's medal in a major European competition began in 1979 when his first club, Fortuna Dusseldorf, were beaten 4–3 by Barcelona in a thrilling Cup Winners' Cup Final in Basle. Allofs scored the second goal, his fourth in the the tournament that season, but it was not enough to stop a strong Barcelona side which included such stars as Dutch maestro Johan Neeskens and powerful Austrian forward Hans Krankel.

At least Aloffs took consolation from the rave reviews he earned in the semi-final defeat of Banik Ostrava—his brace of goals in the first leg proved decisive.

Seven years later, he was on the losing side with Cologne in the UEFA Cup Final against the other Spanish giants, Real Madrid. Once again Allofs found the target in a high-scoring final, but that is where the similarities end. Allofs' goal in the first leg in Madrid was only a consolation—Real scored five times.

The second leg in Cologne attracted a crowd of only 15,000 and they saw the home team salvage some pride with a 2–0 victory—a 5–3 defeat on aggregate.

Here's Allofs on international duty with Germany as they beat Sweden 2–0 in their World Cup qualifying encounter.

It was not a good year for Allofs. He was also in the West German team beaten 3–2 by Argentina in the World Cup Final in Mexico. Valdano, who scored twice for Real Madrid in the UEFA Cup Final, brought back bad memories with Argentina's second goal in the Azteca Stadium.

Allofs did not play in the 1982 World Cup Final when the Germans lost 3–1 to Italy, but he did collect a winner's medal in the 1980 European Championship. West Germany beat surprise finalists Belgium 2–1, with both goals scored by Horst Hrubesch. Arguably the greatest moment in Allofs' career came earlier in the tournament when he claimed a hat-trick in the 3–2 defeat of Holland, which confirmed the end of the Dutch era of brilliance.

The match also marked the emergence on an international scale of one of the most formidable and feared strikers in the 1980s. His finishing power and anticipation in the penalty area set him aside from most striking rivals of that time. It spoke volumes for his ability and durability that he was still around and scoring goals at the highest level twelve years later.

Something had to give in Lisbon in the 1992 Cup Winners' Cup Final—the end of Allofs' search for a winner's medal marked the continuation of the French jinx in European finals. Monaco's defeat was the sixth for French teams in as many final appearances. Monaco dominated the match, but Allofs' inspiration gave the Germans a greater cutting edge in attack and Werder, like their respected striker, enjoyed their first taste of European glory.

The perceived second-class status of the competition was not given a thought amid Werder's victory celebrations. The Cup Winners' Cup is held in high regard in Britain because entry is reserved for winners of the FA Cup. But it is not the case on the continent. It was the last of the three club European tournaments to be introduced and many countries launched cup competitions as a means of cashing in on the Cup Winners' Cup.

However, it would be a crying shame if Allofs' glory were to be tainted by suggestions that his success came in a second-rate competition. He fully deserved the accolades and praise heaped on him in Lisbon. Only the jealous and misguided could dispute his place in a hall of fame for German strikers.

RANGERS' DOUBLE LIFE AFTER SOUNESS

By STEPHEN NAYSMITH *(Glasgow Sports Agency)*

THE year 1992 was one in which it was fashionable to prove yourself to be 'your own man.' And just as John Major was winning himself a mandate which finally cast off the shadow of Margaret Thatcher, Rangers' manager Walter Smith had the satisfaction of steering the Ibrox club to a League and Cup double, a feat they had not achieved in the Graeme Souness era.

When he arrived in 1986, Souness revived Rangers to the extent that they were winning the Premier Division almost as of right and playing virtual monopoly with the Skol Cup tournament. As his assistant, Smith enjoyed only a minor share of the credit. Some wondered whether the momentum could be maintained as Souness headed south to join Liverpool in April 1991, especially under a man so different from his high-profile, combative predecessor.

Smith has more than proved himself, leading Rangers to still more success culminating in the 1991–92 double. Their fourth title in a row, and first Scottish Cup since 1981, amply reinforced their dominance of football north of the border.

Smith came from Dundee United, after a long association with the Tayside club as a defender with a hard-man reputation and then as manager Jim McLean's right-hand man. Even so, he leapt at the chance to partner Souness

Togetherness on the bench as demonstrated by Rangers' manager of the moment, Graeme Souness, and his eventual successor Walter Smith.

THAT'S FOUR IN FOUR YEARS!

WALTER SMITH (left) should feel well pleased as he watches Rangers achieve the League-Cup double in his first season as manager. Richard Gough and Ally McCoist (right) are delighted too with this fourth successive Scottish League title and Rangers' 42nd in all. Sharing the spoils also was Alexei Mikhailichenko (below right), a canny signing by Smith from Sampdoria.

and give him the benefit of his knowledge of Scottish football. As Smith jokes, his former boss gave him in return a taste for the finer things in life—food, wine, success: 'I was a mince-and-potato man until I met Graeme.' When the chance came to take over from his flamboyant predecessor, Smith was ready.

Nobody can say that Smith's quieter style has been ineffective, but he has plenty of ambitions left unfulfilled. Perhaps the most important of these is to see the club becoming a force in European competition. It is certainly something the Ibrox faithful have awaited for a long time, and Smith acknowledges that the club should be making an impact beyond the domestic sphere.

'Europe is becoming more and more a factor,' he says, 'and I don't think we are far away from being able to field a team who can do well outside Scotland.' There are many aspects of Scottish football which would have to change, however, before Scottish teams can match up in Europe, according to the Rangers boss.

Rangers and the other larger clubs have long been arguing for a smaller Premier League and fewer games, to give more time for international matches and to let the fans watch players who are neither injured nor over-tired. Smith

also believes football training in Scotland needs radical improvements.

'We really have to do something if we are to move properly towards the future,' he says. 'We are all looking at a game that is dying. There is no doubt in my mind the standard of young players in the first and second divisions is not good enough. There used to be enough talent to go around, but not now.'

He also feels that change is needed from the bottom up when he says: 'When you go to a kids' match and listen, a lack of commitment is always blamed for defeat. No-one ever says defeat was caused by failure to control or pass the ball.'

This perhaps is the reason why the recent successful Rangers squads have been built around expensive imports from England and abroad. Walters, Kuznetsov and Spackman were signed by Souness and Smith has continued the tradition, bringing Alexei Mikhailichenko from Sampdoria, Dale Gordon from Norwich and Paul Rideout from Notts County.

The number of new faces in the side last season was a worry for Walter Smith and he was pleased that they managed to settle well enough to stay

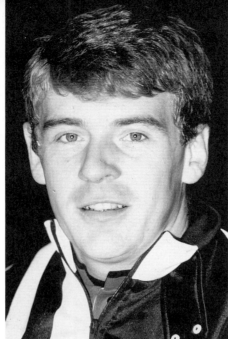

TOP MEN BRING THE TOP PRIZES

ABOVE LEFT Paul Rideout, whose signing from Notts County added to the depth of talent at Ibrox. Sharing the success also was Andy Goram, Scotland's goalkeeper (ABOVE RIGHT), and one wonders how long it will be before Rangers need to enlarge their trophy room, seen here with Graeme Souness on guard duty.

in the championship race in the early part of the season. 'I wondered at that time if having so many newcomers would beat us, but after setbacks in October we dug in and got going again.'

Mikhailichenko was a particular source of worry and many critics thought the Ukrainian's elegant skills would be out of place in the hurly-burly of the Premier Division. Strength and stamina are too often more necessary than skill in this league and talented players have been known to flounder for lack of these attributes.

As the season went on, though, he won the fans over with an ability to turn matches with a flash of brilliance, both making and taking goals. 'He scored good goals and that was vital because he replaced Mark Walters, who was giving us ten or twelve a year,' Smith points out.

Another of the season's revelations was Ally McCoist, who Smith brought back at the age of twenty-nine from a spell on the subs' bench for his most successful season yet. The striker was showered with recognition as he scooped player-of-the-year awards from the Scottish Professional Footballers Association, the Scottish Football Writers and Scottish Brewers and secured the European Golden Boot with his thirty-four league goals, the first Scot to do so.

But the Rangers squad is not impressive in its individual strengths so much as in its depth of talent, with international-class players covering every position. In Andy Goram and Alastair Maxwell they have two of the Scotland squad's goalkeepers, protected by a defence that includes Richard Gough and Gary Stevens as well as David Robertson who, while not yet a Scotland regular, surely will be in time.

Midfield is always an area where Rangers dominate the opposition and with McCall, Spackman and Mikhailichenko it is easy to see why. Perhaps the double

season's happiest story was the return to form of Ian Durrant, whose midfield brilliance had been in doubt following a terrible injury in the 1988–89 season.

Up front, Rangers have a pool of talent which is the envy of managers throughout Britain. With McCoist, Gordon, Hateley, Rideout and Huistra to call upon, it was no surprise when they were the first club in Scotland to net more than one hundred goals in a season.

Although cautious and contemplative by nature, Walter Smith is not afraid to challenge those who run the game when he disagrees with them. A case in point is the ongoing saga of a national stadium for the Scotland team. The Scottish Football Association has considered revamping Hampden or even building an entirely new facility but the money has never been available to do the job properly. Even if it were, according to Smith, it could be better spent.

'People are talking about the need for a national stadium. Why?' he asks. 'Internationals could be played at Ibrox, Pittodrie and wherever Celtic decide to build. Most other countries don't have national stadiums and there is no necessity for us to spend money on one, especially when we are talking about money which could be given to the development of youth football.'

Whatever the 1992–93 season brings for Rangers (and they will be hard pushed to surpass the previous season's achievements) it is clear that their ambitions cannot be limited to the Premier League for much longer. They are always the subject of speculation when suggestions are made for European mini-leagues and British super leagues, and their fans will demand the best competition if they are to continue to flock to Ibrox Stadium.

While the Scottish League structure continues to demand that they play relative minnows such as Airdrie and Falkirk four times a season, it is inevitable that Rangers will eventually look elsewhere for their opposition.

LINEKER

IFB's farewell tribute

to a great England player

and a worthy captain

By GERRY COX
Mail on Sunday

WHEN a living legend decides to hang up his boots, it is usually a sign that he is getting rusty and past his best. But Gary Lineker finished his long and distinguished career in England playing some of his best football, scoring thirty-five goals for Tottenham Hotspur and winning the English football writers' Footballer of the Year award for the second time.

In doing so, he was following in the footsteps of other footballing legends Sir Stanley Matthews, Tom Finney, Danny Blanchflower, Kenny Dalglish and John Barnes. And who would dispute that Lineker does not deserve to be among them?

Lineker's career has been so perfect that one wonders if it was mapped out for him by some higher being. Not only has he risen from modest beginnings to become one of the world's great footballers, he has won admirers all over the world for his impeccable behaviour both on and off the pitch. The fact that he has never been booked or sent off, in spite of going in where it hurts against some of the world's toughest defenders, says volumes about his temperament and, unlike so many of his contemporaries, there has never been so much as a whiff of scandal about him. Gary Lineker is the perfect gentleman

A living legend . . . and the perfect gentleman of football

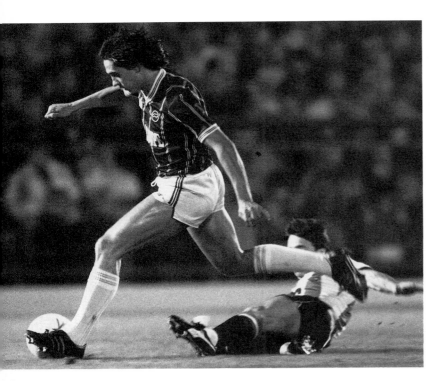

LEICESTER CITY . . . EVERTON . . .

of football and has proved time and time again that nice guys do not always finish second.

It is ironic that the last man to wear the mantle of English football's ambassador to the world so naturally was Bobby Charlton, another former England centre-forward and captain.

Lineker's final ambition for England was to lead them to the European Championship in 1992 and beat Charlton's record of forty-nine goals in 108 games. While Lineker's goals have never been as spectacular as some of Charlton's, it can be argued that he has scored them in a far more defensive era and he has had to work hard to adjust his game.

In his early days, his natural lightning speed — 100 metres in 10.5 seconds — would take him clear of defences. But after a bout of hepatitis in 1988 slowed him down slightly, Lineker had to adapt to making perfectly-timed runs to be in the right place at the right time to meet crosses.

As he has grown older, he has become wiser about his game. He studies videotapes in an effort to improve his output but keeps the secrets of his success to himself.

His almost Corinthian attitude in an increasingly unsportsmanlike game has been invaluable in helping English football's readmission on to the world stage

BARCELONA . . .   TOTTENHAM . . .

after a decade as the pariahs of the game because of hooliganism. Lineker epitomises good health and clean living to such an extent that he was chosen to promote an anti-drugs campaign in Malaysia and South-East Asia.

Ever since making his debut for home club Leicester City in 1979, Lineker has caused more misery for defenders and goalkeepers than just about anybody in British football, yet few have criticised him.

His late burst of seven goals in six games was enough to save Tottenham from the threat of relegation in 1991–92, and it took his season's tally to twenty-eight in thirty-five League games, his best ratio in the League. 'I was pleased to be able to leave on a high note, playing some of my best football and scoring goals,' he said. 'I was delighted with my goal-scoring ratio, because I missed a few games in the last season.'

The reason for that was the serious illness of his baby son George, who was discovered to be suffering from leukaemia when only a few months old, shortly before Christmas 1991. Gary Lineker and his wife Michelle spent many

Peter Beardsley has nothing but praise for his former England teammate Lineker.

TRIBUTES to Gary Lineker's prowess have rained in since he was a teenage scoring sensation, once hitting 161 goals in a season for a boys club.

'He is the hottest property in British football.'—GORDON MILNE, Leicester's manager, in 1985, when Lineker won his first Golden Boot as the First Division's top scorer.

'Lineker is up there with Greaves, Law, Best and Rush.'—BOBBY ROBSON, England manager 1982–90.

'Whenever you have Lineker in your side, you have a chance.'— PETER BEARDSLEY, England team-mate 1986–90.

'Up there with the greats. A fabulous finisher whose England record speaks for itself.'—PETER SHILTON, former England goalkeeper and the world's most-capped footballer.

'He is a genius, and not in the devalued way that is applied to any footballer of talent. It's as if he has taken a degree in the art of goal-scoring. He has a better appreciation of angles than anyone else.'— PETER SHREEVES, Tottenham manager 1991–92.

'The two best strikers in the world are Rudi Voller and Gary Lineker.'—BERTI VOGTS, coach of world champions Germany, in 1992.

anxious nights at their son's hospital bedside as experts administered treatment, to which George responded positively.

The Linekers were inundated with support from well-wishers, and Gary said: 'The supporters have always treated me well but they were especially good over those few months during our personal problems, with their cards and gifts. It was not an easy time and they helped more than they can imagine.'

As well as his family problems, Lineker spent more than a year playing under the shadow of Tottenham's huge financial burden which threatened to bankrupt them before manager Terry Venables bought out the club just weeks after winning a record eighth FA Cup.

Lineker says: 'It was an amazing experience, and not easy for the players or the fans.' Incredibly, that 1991 FA Cup winners medal was Lineker's first success in England. His only other club trophies were winning the Spanish Cup and European Cup Winners Cup in three seasons with Barcelona.

But individual honours have been bestowed throughout his career. It all started to click in 1986 in his first season at Everton after an £800,000 move. He ended as the First Division's top scorer with forty goals, the last of which came in the FA Cup Final defeat by Liverpool.

He was voted Footballer of the Year by both the football writers and his fellow professionals and lined up a dream move to Spanish giants Barcelona. Even better, he became a national hero by helping England to the quarter-finals of the World Cup and returned with the Golden Boot as the tournament's top scorer with six goals.

After three years at Barcelona, in which he ultimately fell out of favour

with coach Johan Cruyff, Lineker returned to England with Tottenham, where he linked up again with former Barcelona coach Terry Venables.

His first season was a typical success as he scored thirty goals and helped England to the semi-final of the World Cup. The following season brought fewer goals but the FA Cup, while he was awarded the OBE in the 1992 New Year's Honours list.

Such was Lineker's standing throughout the land that when he scored against Manchester United in the closing minutes of his final match in the First Division, the opposition supporters at Old Trafford rose with the Spurs fans to give him a standing ovation. It was, as he admitted, an emotional moment. 'I felt a lump in my throat the size of a football.'

With Lineker in such dynamic form, and showing the young pretenders to his throne the way to goal, surely it must have been tempting for him to stay a little longer before setting off to join the new J-League in Japan?

'I am sure I could have carried on in the First Division for a couple more years,' he says, 'but I do not know if I would have been at my best, especially playing sixty or more games a season at such a physical level. I would rather go out with three of my best years behind me than after three years when fans might see me below my best.'

That is typical of Gary Lineker—not allowing his high standards to slip right to the end of his English career.

Happy days for Gary at White Hart Lane, where he learned to cope with the often bizarre tricks of You-know-who.

Here's how we prefer to remember Gary as an England superstar . . .

Gary heads for goal in the 5–0 demolition of Turkey in 1985. Defender Ismail Demirez is left trailing as Lineker rounds off a super hat-trick performance.

Sadly, here's how the Press saw his farewell in Sweden

JEFF POWELL (Daily Mail):
"This time the manager may have gone too far. If, by denying the man who has captained the country with such dignity the last minutes of his illustrious career, Taylor was trying to indicate where the blame should lie, he will find no sympathy among the nation.

"This was no way to treat a hero . . . What he did to Lineker leaves a taste in the mouth more bitter by far than defeat by Sweden and it will take time and wise counsel to revive our appetite for his England team."

STUART JONES (The Times):
"Lineker, the Footballer of the Year who has served his country with such distinction for eight years, deserved better and fairer treatment. That is based not on sentiment but wholly on his contribution to England's most cohesive and brightest half of the tournament.

"While he was there, leading the front line with David Platt's support, the team looked capable of overcoming a cruelly disrupted build-up and reaching the semi-finals. After he had inexplicably been ordered to walk off—and into the retirement he had imposed on himself for the end of this championship—England lost their shape, their discipline and eventually their heart."

STEVE CURRY (Daily Express):
"We yearned for a Gascoigne, sighed for Waddle and needed a Bryan Robson, just someone to stem the rise of the flood water. But no rescue came and Gary Lineker, who has been a lone figure in the tournament waiting for the opportunities that are his lifeline, was disgracefully made the scapegoat."

COLIN GIBSON (Daily Telegraph): "Was it not Lineker, after all, who had converted a slender chance in Poland to bring England here in the first place? And was it not Lineker who had stunned the Germans with only eight minutes remaining in the World Cup semi-finals in Italy two years ago? It was a sad way for Lineker to bow out of international football."

. . . and as Cup hero of Spurs

A moment to savour and one worth waiting for! Lineker holds high the FA Cup after the memorable win against Nottingham Forest in 1991.

Welcome to Japan

—and a few surplises for you, Mr and Mrs Rineker!

GARY Lineker will be in for a surprise or two when he arrives in Japan to play out the twilight of his career with Nagoya Grampus 8.

Although football is played by more people than any other sport in Japan, the Japanese have had semi-professional football only since 1986 and the new 'J' League scheduled to start in April 1993 was to be the country's first professional league.

It is fitting that Lineker should be spearheading the new league because it was an Englishman, a schoolteacher named Johns, who introduced football to Japan in 1874. A national association was formed in 1921, and the Football Association presented a trophy, the English Cup, which was the forerunner of the country's premier knockout competition, the Emperor's Cup.

At national level, Japan's greatest success has been in the Olympic Games, the zenith being third place in the 1968 Mexico Olympics. Yet football has failed to dislodge sumo wrestling and baseball as Japan's most popular spectator sports, especially among the older generations. It is against this back-drop that the 'J' League must try to establish itself.

Lineker's new team, Nagoya Grampus 8, were formerly known as Toyota after the car company which dominates the city of Nagoya and heads the twenty or so sponsors backing the team, including Chubu Electric and Tokai Railway.

One of the problems Japanese teams have faced in trying to attract large support is that fans were previously tied to particular teams by company loyalty.

With Japan hoping to stage the 2002 World Cup finals, it needs to build top-class facilities and show that it is ready to stage a major tournament. Matches against good European and South American sides have drawn reasonable attendances, so the Japanese have decided to invest in leading players from those continents to capture the public's imagination.

Argentinian captain Diego Maradona was top of their shopping list until he was disgraced in a drugs scandal in Italy, after which he was banned from playing football. Lothar Matthaus was another possibility, but a serious injury early in 1992 ruled him out.

No expense has been spared in an effort to make the new league professional in every way. Apart from the estimated £2.5 million it cost them to sign Lineker, Grampus 8 are building a brand-new 30,000 capacity stadium which will cost more than £12 million. Their previous ground was an uncovered space with little or no seating.

They have set aside around £4 million for building proper training facilities in nearby Nisshin and £6 million for running costs, which will include wages, bonuses and administration expenses.

Alongside Lineker will be Brazilians Jorge Putinatti and Rodrigues Edon in a squad composed mostly of Japanese.

Grampus 8 are named after a mythical porpoise-type creature, while eight is a lucky number. They will be hoping for some luck, after Toyota finished bottom of an eight-team league in 1992.

Gary and Michelle Lineker have had their joys and sorrows. Now they head for the great unknown of Japanese football and culture. May theirs be the happiness they deserve.

Much will be expected of Lineker, both on and off the field. Part of his contract will be to advertise Toyota cars, and his image as the perfect gentleman of football will bring him into great demand for adverts and personal appearances.

Not only will he have a difficult language to learn, but he and his family will have to adapt to a very different lifestyle in Japan. Nagoya is a crowded industrial city more than 200 miles from Tokyo, almost two hours' journey on the famous bullet train.

Dominated by the car giant Toyota, Nagoya is a sprawling mass of chemical works, factories and modern buildings. It was rebuilt extensively after being heavily bombed by the Allies during World War II because it was a major armaments centre. It is not known for being a stylish city, which may come as a shock for the Linekers after their millionaire lifestyles in the swishest parts of Barcelona and London.

But the main reason why Gary Lineker was a rare British success when he first played abroad, with Barcelona, was that he and his wife immersed themselves thoroughly in the Spanish culture. If he does the same in Japan, as he intends to, Gary Winston Lineker should become as big a hero in the land of the rising sun as he has been in the rest of the world.

No-one deserves it more.

Managers

VUJADIN BOSKOV

Born: May 9, 1931.
Management career: In SWITZERLAND—Young Boys;
YUGOSLAVIA—Vojvodina; HOLLAND—Ajax,
Feyenoord; SPAIN—Real Zaragoza, Real Madrid,
Sporting Gijon; ITALY—Ascoli, Sampdoria, AS Roma.

THERE are two groups of Yugoslavs who have recently prospered beyond all expectations, regardless of the internal troubles in the country. The precocious, gifted players like Prosinecki and Pancev—and more so, the coaches.

Among the latter are Raddy Antic, who revived Real Madrid, Dragoslav Stepanovic of Eintracht Frankfurt fame, and Bora Milutinovic, the boss of Mexico, Costa Rica and probably the USA in consecutive World Cups. But the jewel in the crown is Vujadin Boskov, the man whose six years at Sampdoria turned them from a good average Italian club into one of the finest in Europe.

In the four years before his move to AS Roma, Sampdoria won the Italian Cup, European Cup Winners Cup, Italian Championship and a place in the European Cup Final.

Boskov, whose teams can be identified by their entertaining style of play, put aside the fortune he will earn from Roma to coach his homeland for the 1992 European Championship. Ironically, they were forced to withdraw in favour of Denmark because of the civil war in Yugoslavia. Previously, he had drifted around Europe and influenced some of the world's finest players.

He started his coaching career way back in 1963 after playing as a wing-half for Yugoslavia in the 1954 World Cup, and has worked his way to the top with a string of league successes. Vojvodina, Real Madrid and finally Sampdoria all won their national titles with Boskov at the helm.

A few words from Stepanovic help to explain what makes Boskov tick. Stepanovic says: 'I think we're from a talented football nation where the people have a great passion for the game and love to express themselves through their football.'

for hire!

men who stand and deliver

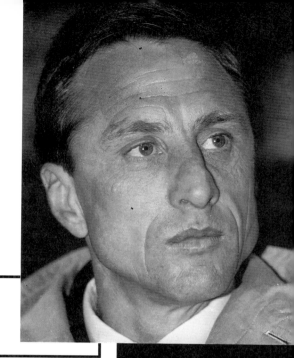

JOHAN CRUYFF

THEY say that managers are a tough breed, and no-one in a football hot seat has shown more resilience than Johan Cruyff, the greatest Dutch footballer of all time.

While a long list of managers in Spain have been sacked like potatoes from Spain's top clubs, Cruyff has kept Barcelona in the top echelon of European football. And when Barcelona stylishly beat Sampdoria to win the 1992 European Cup and complete a full set of European trophies, Cruyff became the hero of Catalonia.

Yet just over a year before the final Cruyff was taken ill and forced to undergo heart surgery. He recovered to retake the reins in time for a vital Cup Winners Cup semi-final against Juventus. Medical evidence has since proved that, rather than becoming a man at the mercy of a heart condition, he is able to handle the stress of top-level football.

During matches, he shows immunity to pressure by maintaining a level heartbeat. What an example he is to the likes of Liverpool manager Graeme Souness, who had a similar operation a year later.

As well as a restructured heart, Cruyff possesses a revered football brain which, in his playing days and as a manager, helped Ajax to win many domestic and European trophies.

His Ajax team won the Cup Winners Cup in 1987, and when he moved to Barcelona, his new team emulated Ajax immediately.

The only prize Cruyff is not likely to win is a popularity contest. His aloof manner, which he finds beneficial in his control of Barcelona's superstars, was evident when he was questioned about managing Holland in the 1994 World Cup.

'I have given my word to the federation,' he said. 'If they need me they can call me. If they have someone better than me, don't call me.'

MANAGERS

JOHN TOSHACK

Born: March 22, 1949.
Management career: in ENGLAND—Swansea City;
SPAIN—Real Sociedad (twice), Real Madrid;
PORTUGAL—Sporting Lisbon.

HE has been shown the door by debt-ridden Swansea City and Spanish giants Real Madrid, yet John Toshack has never failed to bounce back quickly. Now, the former Wales and Liverpool striker is back at Real Sociedad, where he originally confirmed his promise as a manager of the highest order.

Toshack spent four years at Sociedad before joining another Spanish club, Real Madrid, in 1989. Sociedad won the Spanish Cup under Toshack and, in 1987–88, finished as runners-up to mighty Barcelona in the League. These achievements clinched him a £250,000-a-year job in Madrid.

This was a long way from the dark days of 1984, when Welsh club Swansea dismissed Toshack. Several years earlier, he had worked a miracle by taking Swansea from the English Fourth Division to the First Division.

Toshack wasted no time on self-pity when his relationship with Swansea turned sour. He quickly established himself in Portugal for a year with Sporting Lisbon.

As a player, he occasionally had to win over critics of his style by scoring goals—but he stuck steadfastly to his methods and he succeeded. As a manager, he is equally single-minded, and the fanatical Basque supporters of Sociedad have finally had to accept football more familiar in Britain than on the continent.

When Real Madrid failed to win the European Cup, it cost Toshack his job, but Sociedad are more flexible . . . as long as results remain good. And Toshack usually gets results.

Perhaps that is why another of Europe's top clubs, Liverpool, are said to be 'interested' in Toshack whenever the management position is vacant. Maybe he will return to Anfield one day, but for now he is happy to reign in Spain.

FOR HIRE

BOBBY ROBSON

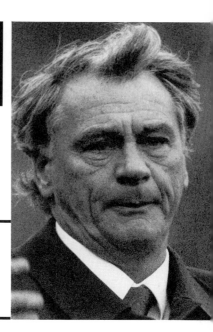

Born: February 18, 1933
Management career: In ENGLAND—Fulham, Ipswich
Town, national team; HOLLAND—PSV Eindhoven;
PORTUGAL—Sporting Lisbon.

BOBBY Robson seems determined to prove that there is life after being manager of England. He is thriving away from the intense pressure that comes with running a national team.

Although his record over eight years in the England job is impressive, the weight of public and media demand often left him looking tired and burdened. Poor relations with the Press, especially when his private life came under the spotlight, overshadowed some of his achievements.

In Mexico 1986, his team was unlucky to be knocked out of the World Cup in the quarter-finals, by Argentina. Next time round, he was the first manager to take England to a World Cup semi-final on foreign soil. In between, Robson, who won 20 England caps as a player, steered England to an unbeaten run lasting for two years.

When he vacated the England job, it was ironic he settled in Holland, after he had been forced to plot the downfall of their national team in the 1988 European Championship and 1990 World Cup.

The Dutch fans may have remembered Robson from 1981, when he led Ipswich to a glorious UEFA Cup triumph over AZ67 Alkmaar of Holland, three years after winning the FA Cup with Ipswich. He had also taken exciting Dutch midfielders to English football, in Arnold Muhren and Frans Thyssen.

He had no joy in European competition with PSV Eindhoven, but by winning the Dutch championship in both his seasons there, gave a reminder of the management skills that served Ipswich so well for thirteen years.

If Robson completes a hat-trick of league titles in Portugal it could be quite an achievement—for on his arrival, Sporting Lisbon had not won the Portuguese League in over ten years.

HAT-TRICKS COMPLETE!

But Ajax and Barcelona can forget the honeymoon, says NICK CALLOW

THE history-making players of Ajax and Barcelona may still not have achieved enough to satisfy the insatiable appetites of their supporters and presidents. The Dutch and Spanish sides kicked off the 1992 European Championship summer displaying the best that the continental game has to offer and, in doing so, joined Juventus as the most successful sides in European club competition.

Before Ajax won the UEFA Cup against Torino, and Barcelona lifted the European Cup after beating Sampdoria, only the mighty Italians could lay claim to all three European club competitions. The danger is, however, that the Dutch masters from Amsterdam and the skilled Spaniards of Catalonia spend too long in celebration.

Johan Cruyff has played for and managed both clubs and joins a highly-select group of footballers who have won the European Cup as player, with Ajax, and as manager, with Barcelona. Nobody knows better the demands and expectations of Europe's new kings. Speaking in the build-up to Barcelona's

ABOVE The victory march begins for Ajax, 1992 winners of the UEFA Cup, with Aron Winter (left) and skipper Danny Blind showing the way.
OPPOSITE The king of the free-kick specialists has done it again! And Ronald Koeman knows it's the winner for Barcelona in the European Cup Final.

historic 1992 Wembley win over Sampdoria, Cruyff explained what winning means to him and the two clubs that worship him: 'I have all kinds of ambitions stemming from the main ambition of wanting to win. If you are trying to succeed you need incentives, you have to change things all the time. You can't stop and congratulate yourself because, as soon as you do, it's over.'

Winning the European Cup meant everything to Barcelona. Cruyff, who reportedly was paid £1.4 million-a-year to gain that success, received a £500,000 bonus for winning at Wembley, and the players were on £150,000-a-man. But leading into the final, doubts about Cruyff's ability reached new heights as disgruntled supporters questioned his team selection and they resented his speculated move to manage the Dutch national side, whatever the outcome.

They also found little comfort from his utterances at that time. 'It is not certain I will stay here,' he said. 'Barcelona is a volatile club, very volatile.

Showing a leg is Sonny Silooy (Ajax) as he takes on Gianluigi Lentini (Torino) in their tense UEFA Cup second-leg battle. A few weeks later, Lentini was to join the already talent-loaded ranks of AC Milan for an astronomical price of £15.6 million—£9 million for the transfer and £6.6 million spread over four years for the player.

Things are wrong, little things that to an outsider are very difficult to explain, but things are erratic. It's something to do with the mentality here, the character of the people and the way they work.'

The club has 100,000 members and an all-powerful president in José Luis Nunez. They cause the sort of pressure that led to the normally phlegmatic Cruyff requiring a heart-by-pass operation at the start of 1991. 'I had to choose between tobacco and football and I chose football,' he said. His forty-cigarettes-a-day habit had not helped ease the demands of the fans.

Wembley, the scene of Cruyff's first European Cup win with Ajax, proved a fitting stage for the final. More than anything, to the supporters, this win meant they could now taunt their arch-rivals Read Madrid on an almost equal footing, as long as they chose to forget that the enemy have lifted the Champions Club Cup on six occasions. Barcelona had reached the final twice before; in 1961 against Benfica and in 1986, with Terry Venables in charge, when they lost to Steaua Bucharest.

It was Cruyff's countryman, Ronald Koeman, who delivered the booming free-kick which won the final in extra time. Cruyff had signed Koeman from Ajax when he took over in Spain and therein lies another tale of potential woe back in Amsterdam. Ajax may have pipped Barcelona to second place in the ruling European triumvirate, but the demands for success continue to weigh heavily on the players and managers who pass through the club.

For a team with such tradition in excellence and entertainment, Ajax have always struggled to impress their supporters and the people of Amsterdam, let alone their own players. Even during Cruyff's playing heyday of the seventies, when they won the European Cup three times in succession, attendances dipped to as low as 8,000 and they were once booed after winning 5–0 because they had failed to play with sufficient flair. Amsterdam is an exotic city with entertainment at the top of priorities and the football team has to mirror the charismatic lifestyle.

These pressures, and the club's inability to match the likes of Barcelona on financial terms, has resulted in a string of world-class talent leaving the club before reaching their peak. By the end of the 1971–72 season Cruyff's side had won thirty of their thirty-four League games, yet by 1973 the era was over. Cruyff was sensationally voted out of the club's captaincy by his team-mates and the great man went to Barcelona. That heralded the demise of the side that coined the phrase 'Total Football'. Wim Suurbier, Johan Neeskens and Ruud Krol all left in quick succession.

In 1981 Cruyff made a dramatic return to Amsterdam, facing the consequences of cavalier investments in three years of retirement. Until he left again in 1983 for arch-rivals Feyenoord, with money again the stumbling block, Cruyff continued to amaze spectators with his skill. During that time the club was tutoring the likes of Marco van Basten, Frank Rijkaard and Gerald Vanenburg. They, like Cruyff, all soon left for richer climates.

Even during their triumphant season of 1991–92, manager Leo Beenhakker was lured to Spanish side Real Madrid. And replacement Louis Van Gaal, as

Leo Beenhakker was on top of the world as manager of Ajax, but the lure of Spain and Real Madrid was irresistible.

Cruyff pointed out, could not afford to enjoy the UEFA Cup win for too long. The sad inevitability was that he knew that the new crop of Ajax stars, including Bryan Roy and Holland's Player of the Year Dennis Bergkamp, would, at some stage, be tempted by the lure of the lire or the pull of the peseta.

Ajax's European achievements must be applauded, especially after crowd trouble ended with UEFA ordering them to play the first three rounds away from home, following a total ban the season before, but they can forget a honeymoon period—in the pursuit of excellence, there is no such thing.

Together, Ajax and Barcelona could probably fill the combined trophy rooms of the entire English Premier League, barring Liverpool, but the latest protagonists at the two clubs have learned to accept living life by a code of 'here today, gone tomorrow'.

Barcelona have completed their European hat-trick and Ronald Koeman sets off with Michael Laudrup to salute their loyal fans at Wembley.

The simple code of Mr Milan

'Nobody works for Berlusconi; everyone works with Berlusconi'

By MARK DEMUTH (Sunday Express)

MILAN president Silvio Berlusconi contradicts the popular view that no single individual is larger than a club. In simple terms Berlusconi is Mr Milan.

The finest side in Europe is a creation of the wealth and vision of its multimillionaire owner. It would be futile to suggest otherwise. His involvement and influence permeates all areas.

Milan has always been a top club, but not on the scale of its present ranking on the world stage. The rich history and success since formation in 1899 provided a solid background for Berlusconi when he bought control. He has built on that platform.

Milan have won the European Cup, World Club Championship and the

Marco Van Basten, here in action for AC Milan, has been told by Berlusconi that he can stay with the club for the rest of his career if he so chooses.

Italian Championship twice each since Berlusconi came to their rescue when they were on the brink of collapse six years ago.

The club was £15 million in debt, the previous president had fled to South Africa and the players were caught in the middle of a match-fixing scandal. Berlusconi's £20 million investment paid off all the debts and financed the signings of the Dutch triumvirate Ruud Gullit, Marco Van Basten and Frank Rijkaard, who set the Milan pulses racing in the late 1980s.

Berlusconi's business interests stretch far and wide. Milan is the focal point of his empire, although the club represents only the tip of the iceberg.

First and foremost he is a media magnate and is firmly entrenched in the television and newspaper industry. He owns the daily *Il Giornale* newspaper and the Canale 5 television channel. Add to that list his construction companies, insurance houses and supermarket and chains and it is just about impossible to live in Italy and avoid the Berlusconi connection.

However, football—and Milan in particular—is his driving passion and one which never leaves him satisfied. His determination to make Milan the greatest club in the world knows no bounds and Berlusconi made his intentions clear in a whirlwind of transfer activity in the 1992 close season.

Not content with the Dutch trio of Gullit, Van Basten and Rijkaard, Milan's three permitted imports, Berlusconi began stockpiling more foreign players in accordance with the gradual relaxation in Italian import restrictions. In came French and Marseille striker Jean-Pierre Papin, outstanding Yugoslavian Dejan Savicevic and Croat midfielder Zvonimir Boban, and world-record signing Gianluigi Lentini from Torino. But Berlusconi soon dismissed the notion that their arrival would spark the departure of his Dutch internationals.

He said: 'Because we want to sign more foreigners does not mean that we are dissatisfied with any that we already have. We want Gullit, Van Basten and Rijkaard to stay as long as they want—hopefully up until the end of their careers. They have played a very important part in Milan's revival. We respect them as men and we are grateful to them as players.'

Berlusconi is the man most likely to spearhead the creation of a European Super League and he has made no bones about his plans for the 1990s. He outlined in detail his hopes and aspirations soon after Milan clinched the Italian Championship in 1992.

He says: 'In the 1992–93 season Milan will play twice every week. On Sundays in the Italian League; on Wednesday in the European Cup or Italian Cup or television friendlies. This is why we must strengthen our squad. In my six years as president I have never seen our best team play—except in my head. Someone is always injured, or ill, or suspended. So we need many quality players and they accept this.

'The future belongs to the great clubs such as Milan, Real Madrid and Barcelona and all of them playing at least eighty games a season.

'The European cups have become a historical anachronism. It's economic nonsense that a club such as Milan might be eliminated in the first round. A European Cup that lasts the whole season is what Europe wants. After all,

Europe wanted an economic community, with monetary union and a customs union. It's inevitable it should want a football union, too.'

The formation of such an 'elite' League would be worth vast sums of money to those competing, and Berlusconi has already pinpointed the biggest source of income for such a venture. Television—and in particular subscription TV.

'Milan are my laboratory for the future. We have to reach the audience beyond the stadium and that means television,' he says. 'Television represents the theatre of the global village. Milan must be a part of that and would like to be the best. But at the highest level, winning or losing is often a matter of luck. What is important is that we are among the main actors in the theatre.

'Football is currently ignoring part of its audience. First are the fans in the stadium, but that means only 50,000. Then there are the fans who watch bits and pieces of soccer on the states channels. But the third audience, which we are not reaching, is to be found on pay-television.

'In the region around Milan that could mean two or three million new viewers. The latest figures suggest we have five million fans throughout the country. They cannot all get into the stadium—but they could watch on pay-TV.'

Berlusconi prides himself on his man-management skills. He likes to think he is more than a club president to his players at Milan—he is their friend and confidante. He offered an insight into his dealings when it was revealed that Van Basten was party to discussions on who should be signed as his new striking partner. Accordingly, Van Basten's approval was secured before Papin arrived.

The shock appointment of Arrigo Sacchi as Milan coach soon after his arrival was one of the shrewdest moves by Berlusconi. Sceptics doubted Sacchi's ability to cope with the demands placed on him at San Siro, after moving from the relative obscurity of Second Division Parma, but Sacchi was an unqualified success. He steered Milan to their European Cup triumphs in 1989 and 1990 and won plaudits for the stylish football with which his side became associated. He left in the summer of 1991 to become the Italian coach.

Berlusconi says of his managerial ability: 'I must be doing something right. In my companies we went from zero employees to 36,000 employees in a comparatively short time.

'Nobody works for Berlusconi; everyone works with Berlusconi. Managing a football club is not that different from managing any other form of business. You need to choose the right people with the right attitude.

'I approach football in the same manner. That is why Marco Van Basten was fully consulted when it came to choosing who plays alongside him in attack.'

'Sacchi was an unqualified success'

Here's yet another of Berlusconi's superstar signings, Dejan Savicevic, the Yugoslav from Red Star Belgrade.

With Van Basten and Papin in tandem, Milan were planning a concerted attempt for the Champions' Cup after their return to European competition in the 1992–93 season.

Milan had been suspended from Europe the previous season for walking off the pitch in protest after a floodlight failure in the second leg of their European Cup quarter-final defeat by Papin's Marseille in 1991. It was a shameful scene and a disappointing conclusion to their bid for a third successive European Cup title.

Milan were desperate to make amends and the players knew that Berlusconi would not settle for anything but a triumph in 1993.

THE NEW BREED OF SOCCER TALENT

'IF you're good enough, you're old enough' seems to be the motto of British soccer scouts in the Nineties. The search for young talent is the theme of this IFB special article, with JOHN PRICE, schools soccer correspondent of The Daily Telegraph, spotlighting two remarkable youngsters.

TWO UNLIKELY

LADS TO NOTE

THE Public Schools of Forest and Lancing College were the unlikely fostering grounds in 1992 for two talented fifteen-year-olds who could become super-stars in the late 1990s.

Stewart Robson, who attended Brentwood in Essex and went on to play for Arsenal, West Ham and Coventry, is the only former public schoolboy to become a top-class player in recent times. Quinton Fortune and Hisao Iijima are attempting to follow that rarely-used path.

Of the two, Fortune attracted greater public attention because North London giants Tottenham brought him from South Africa in September 1991 and paid for him to attend the £4,000-a-year Forest School in Walthamstow.

Like the Ghanaian Nii Lamptey, another boy wonder who left Africa as a fourteen-year-old to seek fame, Fortune, one of a family of six, was clearly born to play football.

Spurs wanted to sign Nii (it means 'king') but they were beaten to him by Belgian club Anderlecht. They were determined not to miss out this time.

John Moncur, Tottenham's youth development officer, explains: 'He was recommended to Terry Venables by his old Chelsea and England team-mate Barry Bridges, who now lives in South Africa.

'Quinton wanted to continue his football at a higher level and gain a better education than was possible at home. He comes from a township in Capetown and learned his football on the streets. Potentially he is one of the best prospects I've ever seen. If he had been a British youngster there would have been a war between the big clubs to get him.'

Spurs, understandably perhaps, are keen to play down the situation with

THE NEW BREED OF SOCCER TALENT

Fortune, whom they have signed on associate schoolboy forms. Moncur says: 'We're very glad he is with us, but it's too early to say whether he'll make it. I've seen so many talented kids fall away. The difference between him and the Anderlecht boy is that Lamptey had already played for his country in a mini World Cup at Under-17 level. Quinton's done nothing.'

However, Fortune's discoverer, Colin Gie, the Under-16 coach of Western Province and South Africa, had no doubts that his protegé will go to the top. 'Quinton's built like a nineteen-year-old,' he says. 'He'll be in the Premier League at sixteen and become a world star. I've never seen such a talent. Like John Barnes, he can play wide left, left midfield or create havoc through the middle. He's strong and has pace.'

Iijima, from Yokohama, played for the junior club of Nissan until his father, a technician with the Mitsubishi Corporation, sent him to England. He joined Lancing at almost the same time as Fortune arrived at Forest School. A striker with great speed off the mark and immaculate close control, Iijima finished as Lancing's top scorer with fourteen goals in ten first-eleven games, including a hat-trick on his debut. Christ Metcalf, Lancing's master-in-charge, describes him as 'the best schoolboy player I've ever seen.'

Reports of the youngster's exploits quickly spread and, before the end of the 1991–92 season, he had trained with League clubs Brighton and Watford. Brighton coach Ted Streeter says Iijima is 'an exciting prospect—very strong for his age and very technical. He looks small but is better than he looks in the air.'

For now, Fortune and Iijima will remain in the relative anonymity of schools football, playing matches in front of a dozen or so spectators, but do not be at all surprised if, in a few years' time, their names are being chanted at League grounds up and down the country.

Stewart Robson, of Coventry City, is among the few ex-public schoolboys to have become professionals in the Football League.

THE NEW BREED OF SOCCER TALENT

An exhausting day at the school of excellence

THE national school of excellence at Lilleshall, due to close in 1994, has placed as much emphasis on academic achievement as football coaching. Set up in 1984, it has been described as a football boarding school, with a yearly intake of sixteen of the best fourteen-year-olds in the country on two-year scholarships.

Getting into the school has not been easy. Of the 5,000 or so boys signed to centres of excellence around the country, the most promising are put up for initial selection trials. Three-hundred-and-fifty progress to regional trials, to be assessed by FA coaches.

The top forty-five are then invited for a three-day visit to Lilleshall, before this is whittled down to thirty and then a final group of sixteen are selected.

Graham Stuart, Chelsea's England Under-21 midfielder, was among the second year's intake. Here is his account of a typical day at the school.

- *7.30 am—'Up early to shower and get ready for the day.*
- *8.15 am—Breakfast at Lilleshall.*
- *8.45 am—Catch the school bus for a six-mile journey to Idsall Comprehensive, near Newport, Shropshire, for a normal day's school lessons.*
- *3.30 pm—Finish school and return to Lilleshall.*
- *4.00 pm—Prepare for training.*
- *4.30 pm—Out on the training ground under the chief coach for one-and-a-half hour's training. One evening a week will be spent in the gym doing circuit training.*
- *6.00 pm—Finish training, shower and prepare for dinner.*
- *7.00 pm—Dinner.*
- *8.00 pm—Homework hour, doing schoolwork or revising.*
- *9.00 pm—Finish for the day. Short time for relaxation before going to bed—exhausted!'*

One morning a week, when the rest of the pupils at Idsall Comprehensive play games, the FA boys remain at Lilleshall for extra training sessions.

Graham Stuart, the talented Chelsea midfield player, served a gruelling apprenticeship at the national school of excellence.

There's nothing Irish about Jones . . .

By CHRIS DIGHTON, *Sunday Times)*

ABOVE Chelsea autograph-hunters are always welcome with Vinnie Jones, who dreams in vain of joining Big Jack's Irish Brigade.

OPPOSITE Vinnie's teammate at Stamford Bridge, Andy Townsend, has won numerous caps with the Republic, having been born in the lovely Irish town of Maidstone.

IMAGINE being asked to deliver an important letter to the Republic of Ireland team dressing-room and being told that the only way it can be located is by listening at various doors along a dark corridor of the stadium for the distinctive Irish accent.

To the unwitting it would be almost an impossible task, especially if they were to stand, ear cocked against the door, as the Republic of Ireland team manager Jack Charlton—all flat vowels of north-country England—was motivating his men.

Confusion could then possibly turn to madness if Andy Townsend—born in Maidstone, Kent, and sometimes captain of the side—were to add his two-pennyworth in the unmistakable tones of the mutilated vowels of south London.

The point of this is not some exercise in linguistic snobbery but to indicate that the Republic of Ireland is not a team of Irishmen but of footballing mercenaries born of necessity rather than Irish heritage.

Take a recent random match, against the USA which the Republic won 4–1. They started with a team which contained only four men born on home soil—the rest came from London, Birmingham, Glasgow, Manchester and Cornwall.

Of course place of birth does not immediately confer nationality—that can be determined by parents—but in an effort to broaden their choice, Ireland

and Wales have been digging deeper and deeper into the roots of family trees and uncovering all manner of ancestral vices.

The fact is that both Wales and the Republic of Ireland are constantly trying the loaves-and-fishes trick without the miracle. Just how far can a little talent be spread in the world of international football?

FIFA set out the rules of qualification on the basis that a player can play for the country where he is a citizen, provided he fulfils the laws of that country for citizenship.

A spokesman for the FA in London confirms that the yardstick for England is based on Home Office qualifications and a player can adopt the country of birth or of his parents. He says: 'Of course the Republic of Ireland's rules for citizenship may extend back to place of birth of the grandparents; it is a matter for each nation. If, however, England were to adopt that policy, we could end up with a situation where nearly all the players in the world were eligible.'

Another side to the qualification business is that players unlikely to play for England can look to other lands for international honours. During the 1991–92 season, the Chelsea player Vinnie Jones went in search of an Irish grandparent he thought he had but was unable to trace the relevant birth certificate and so his international ambitions were lost.

What Jack Charlton has achieved with the Republic of Ireland is an effective unit welded together from a variety of surprising sources. His successes have come in the World Cup. Wales, on the other hand, have not been so successful. They lost their opening qualification match for the 1994 tournament by losing 5–1 to Romania.

The irony of this British 'go anywhere, play for anyone,' stance is that it is happening at a time when fierce local pride is burning in the hearts of players throughout the world. Yugoslavia has become either Croatia or Serbia and presumably weakened, while the identity of the USSR has vanished in the partisan pride of the Soviet republics. Perhaps that is an avenue yet to be explored by those international cap-hungry English players.

You cannot blame players for wanting to play international football or countries wanting to play them—but surely the line must be drawn somewhere.

PETER the

GOALKEEPERS, Brian Clough once said in praise of Peter Shilton, can be the difference between champions and also-rans. That is why Manchester United manager Alex Ferguson reckons the £600,000 he spent on Peter Schmeichel represents a bargain.

Schmeichel is everything you would expect of a Dane. He is big, blond, assertive and aggressive. He is also establishing himself as one of the best goalkeepers in English football.

Schmeichel is much more than a shot-stopper. His vision and his ability to distribute the ball accurately have added another option to United's potent attack.

'Our goalkeeping coach, Alan Hodgkinson, has no doubt that Schmeichel is the best in the country,' said Mr Ferguson. 'People are saying that Peter could be the best at Old Trafford since Harry Gregg. That's a tremendous compliment to the boy's achievements in his first season in English football and I'm convinced he can become even better.'

Mr Ferguson has been a fan of Schmeichel for four years, but it was not until August 1991 that he could persuade Denmark's top club, Brondby, to accept an offer.

'We tried to sign him in the summer that we bought Jim Leighton from Aberdeen, but the money Brondby were asking was out of the question,' said Mr Ferguson. 'But we didn't forget about him.'

Throughout the 1990–91 season, United watched Schmeichel regularly as Brondby won the Danish title for the fourth time in five years and reached the semi-finals of the UEFA Cup.

'The reports we received on him were excellent and his contract was also

Profile by COLIN GIBSON *(The Daily Telegraph)*

Great Dane

'He's big, blond, assertive and aggressive'

Ferguson says: Peter could be United's best since Gregg

coming to an end. It also helped that he was desperate to play for Manchester United.'

English football can be a culture shock, and there was an element of risk in Schmeichel's decision to move. He had become Denmark's most popular footballer, outstripping the likes of Michael Laudrup, and suddenly every boy in Copenhagen wants to play in goal.

Hans Christian Blm, leading sports writer of Denmark's most successful tabloid, believes his newspaper measures Schmeichel's popularity in sales figures. 'Whenever we have his picture on the front page, our circulation increases,' said Blm. 'He is the most recognisable sportsman in Denmark.'

With most United matches televised in Scandinavia, his fans can easily keep track of his progress. The Danish Press Agency have engaged a Manchester journalist to send reports purely on the goalkeeper.

Schmeichel's first club was Hero, where he played centre-forward. 'When the goalkeeper did not turn up one day, I was the biggest so I went in goal,' he said.

The team were managed by Sven Aag Hansen, who was later to become his father-in-law. 'If Peter had a problem it was his temperament. He was tough to handle,' said Hansen, who would have been delighted to see the Dane acting as peacemaker in the volatile Manchester derby at Old Trafford early in 1992.

But the intensity still exists in Schmeichel's pre-match preparations. 'Don't even bother speaking to him for twenty-four hours before a match,' was the advice of a Danish team-mate.

It is part of his search for perfection, according to Mr Ferguson, who is delighted at the way Schmeichel has adapted to life in England.

'When goalkeepers come to England they often have a problem with the physical side of the game and dealing with the vast number of crosses,' said Mr Ferguson.

Within six matches of his signing for United, Schmeichel had been exposed to the Wimbledon approach and survived.

'It takes some getting used to,' said the Dane. 'Forwards hit you at every opportunity and my problem was to remember to expect physical contact. But I like the competitive edge in English football.' And United believe they have acquired one of the most secure and dominant goalkeepers in the League.

'He gives the whole defence confidence,' said Mr Ferguson. 'They know that even if a forward gets past them, the striker is faced with this massive Dane racing out to confront him.

'I think Neville Southall has been the best goalkeeper in England for a long time, but now he has been joined by others like David Seaman, Tony Coton and Chris Woods.

'I would put Schmeichel in that group and at twenty-seven he still has a lot of time to improve.'

It seems United's future is in good hands.

● *The Editor thanks The Daily Telegraph for permission to reproduce this article.*

ALL TOGETHER NOW... WE ARE THE CHAMPIONS!

THE inevitable first question asked after Howard Wilkinson had guided Leeds United to the 1992 English First Division title was: How does today's Leeds compare with the team of a generation ago?

Comparisons between past and present sides have become a pastime of football fans and commentators in England. Liverpool, Arsenal and Manchester United are regularly scrutinised; now it is the turn of Leeds to go under the

By STEPHEN DAVIES

microscope, which means comparing Wilkinson's side to the legendary team under Don Revie which won two Championships, two Fairs Cups, the FA Cup and League Cup between 1968 and 1974.

The one obvious parallel between the two eras is that both sides emerged suddenly, born from the ashes of average teams.

Revie, like Wilkinson, was a top-quality coach who encouraged young talent and both men were blessed with an uncanny skill in the transfer market. They were not afraid to produce the cheque book in order to satisfy their insatiable desire for success.

Comparisons can be made between players as well. The midfield generals of the respective sides, Johnny Giles and Gordon Strachan, were both signed for bargain sums from Manchester United. Giles was the pivot, the inspiration—and Strachan assumes the same function.

Billy Bremner and David Batty, each of similar height, build and temperament, grew up quickly in the Elland Road cauldron, developing into mature international players.

Jack Charlton and Norman Hunter were an impenetrable and uncompromising pairing at the heart of the defence; in 1992, Chris Fairclough and Chris Whyte developed into an equally tenacious partnership.

Terry Cooper and Tony Dorigo at left-back; Paul Reaney and Mel Sterland at right-back; even Mick Jones and Lee Chapman as the target men up front. There are similarities across the pitch.

The growth of both sides was also along similar lines.

Revie arrived at Elland Road in 1961 to take over a side that had spent most of the post-war period in the Second Division. He embarked on a far-reaching rebuilding programme and in doing so changed the face of English football. For Revie may have turned Leeds into one of the legendary sides in the English game but he was also charged with developing a ruthless and abrasive attitude which won very few friends outside of the city.

Cynical tackles, off-the-ball incidents (even off-the-pitch incidents) punctuated their evolution and they were content to win matches by grinding down the opposition and exposing sides at set-pieces.

It was only after the silverware had started to pile up in the boardroom that their style became more refined. These renowned hard men demonstrated the rest of their repertoire and some of the passing movements were both incisive and mesmerising, akin to the game that flourishes among the best of today's Italian sides.

Wilkinson, like Revie, took over a side that had to muscle its way out of the Second Division. Wilkinson took over in October 1988 with the club languishing at the foot of the Second Division. He immediately spent £300,000 on Strachan and £500,000 for Fairclough.

Those transfers helped to keep Leeds up and, in the summer of 1989, he bought the 'workmen' needed to win promotion—Mel Sterland from Glasgow Rangers and, notably, Vinnie Jones, the notorious hod-carrier-turned-footballer from Wimbledon.

Promotion was achieved and Wilkinson began stage three of his grand plan—winning the Championship. Jones, for example, was now surplus to requirements and he was sold to Sheffield United for £700,000 and a quick profit of £50,000.

Goalkeeper John Lukic and midfielder Gary McAllister, from Arsenal and Leicester respectively, were signed for £1 million apiece while Whyte came from West Brom for a cut-price £450,000.

Their first season back in the First Division ended in a respectable fourth place and in May 1992, twelve months on, they were champions, pipping Manchester United for the title.

And so, a generation on, the famous name of Leeds is back among the continent's elite playing in the European Cup, rubbing shoulders with the likes of AC Milan, Marseille and PSV Eindhoven.

Comparing the two eras will continue while Leeds rule the roost in England

'They grew up quickly in the Elland Road cauldron'

Billy Bremner (left) and David Batty, internationals both and similarly tigerish in style, matured rapidly at the Leeds soccer academy.

but it is worth learning the views of people who have studied both sides at close quarters.

Allan Clarke, for example, was a player at Elland Road from 1969–77 and later managed the club. He is full of praise for the work done by Wilkinson but refuses to accept that there will ever again be a side like the one he was privileged to play in.

'I don't think Leeds will ever see again as strong a squad as the one Don Revie built. It was a one-off, the kind of rarity seen only once in a lifetime. We had a genuinely great, great side with eleven internationals playing every game. And there would be five internationals on the sidelines who couldn't even get a match.'

Former Scottish international Billy Bremner agrees. The flame-haired midfielder spent almost two decades as a Leeds player and was Wilkinson's immediate predecessor as manager. Bremner reckons that Leeds have still more to prove.

'I'm thrilled for Howard but the hardest job in football is not winning the title but maintaining success and that is something that very few managers achieve. The great managers, like Don Revie, stayed at their clubs and were successful for many years.'

Johnny Giles, who finished his eleven-year playing career at Leeds by helping the club win the 1974 Championship, accepts that it is difficult to draw comparisons. He says: 'To be honest, I have to say that in many respects the old team was much superior but there were many reasons for this.

'Revie had brought nine of his champions of 1969 through the ranks. Today Howard Wilkinson cannot lay out his plans as Revie did. Under today's system, Revie would have had a nightmare as richer clubs ran their eyes over his young talent. Imagine the agents who would have been flocking around Elland Road

Jack Charlton in action for the old Leeds invincibles. He and Norman Hunter formed 'an impenetrable and uncompromising pairing' says Stephen Davies.

with the idea of snapping up players like Norman Hunter, Eddie Gray or Peter Lorimer.'

There, in the words of the respected Giles, lies the dichotomy. Times have changed and it is difficult and unfair to compare two such contrasting eras. What can be said is that Wilkinson has worked a miracle at Elland Road, lifting Leeds from the lower reaches of the Second Division to the First Division Championship in less than four years.

At Elland Road, they do not care if the team of the 1960s was better than the team of the 1990s. They are simply delighted that, after a generation in the soccer wilderness, the good times are back.

Lee Chapman (above), the striker supreme in the Leeds Championship-winning team of 1991–92, revived memories of Mick Jones of the old brigade.

See how they fly!

They're generations apart but theirs is a common aim—to mesmerise the opposition in the cause of Manchester United. On the left, teenage star Ryan Giggs; above, the left-wing magician George Best.

S OFF TO A SWING ON THE WING

By MARK DEMUTH

A CLUTCH of gifted wingers was the star attraction when the new English Premier League began in a blaze of publicity in August 1992.

England were dubbed 'wingless wonders' when Sir Alf Ramsey's team swept to World Cup triumph in 1966, but wingers, that exciting breed of talented individuals, were in the vanguard as English football embarked on an historic season in 1992.

Some of the best prospects in the land plied their trade in isolation near the touchline. Give them the ball and space to attack and they would send the temperature soaring, their pace and skill allied to that rarest of qualities in modern-day football—the ability to take on players and beat them. There can be no finer sight in football than a winger in full cry.

The English crowds soon warmed to their efforts. They began to realise just what they had been missing since the winger went into hibernation in the post-Ramsey era.

There was a time when the star turn in each club was a winger. It had not quite reached that degree with the advent of the Premier League, but the success of some of the most successful exponents of wing play greatly enhanced the standing of their profession.

Leading the 'winger' fight-back were such stars as the Manchester United trio Ryan Giggs, Lee Sharpe and Andrei Kanchelskis, Aston Villa and England's Tony Daley, Liverpool's Steve McManaman, John Salako at Crystal Palace, Spurs' £1.75 million signing Darren Anderton and Anders Limpar of Arsenal.

McManaman is arguably the best of the bunch. Giggs caused a stir as Manchester United ran Leeds so close to the League Championship in 1992, but McManaman showed enough potential in Liverpool's FA Cup run to suggest he could be the player of the 1990s.

McManaman's flair and big-match composure were the main features of Liverpool's FA Cup success in 1992. Not only did his switch from the left to right flank turn the Final Liverpool's way against Sunderland, but he scored vital goals en route to Wembley.

McManaman kept Liverpool in the FA Cup virtually single-handed in tough ties against Second Division sides Bristol Rovers and Ipswich Town. He scored decisive goals in the replays against both clubs and his ability gradually wore down their resistance.

Former England midfield maestro Trevor Brooking said of McManaman's match-winning display against Sunderland in the Final: 'He has the unique gift of drifting past defenders effortlessly and Sunderland never managed to

Two flying wingers from foreign parts who have captivated English audiences—Anders Limpar of Arsenal and, right, Andrei Kanchelskis of Manchester United.

cope with his darting runs. He often dragged two or three defenders over to help cope with him.

'McManaman's skill compensated for the absence of John Barnes through injury and he and Liverpool full-back Rob Jones down the right augurs well for a future England partnership.'

One player for whom the 1991–92 season was supposed to be extra special was Palace winger John Salako. He was the outstanding success of England's 1991 tour of Australasia when manager Graham Taylor gave him his international debut.

Salako returned home with praise ringing in his ears. Taylor picked him for the prestigious friendly against Germany at Wembley, but he went off with a knee injury after colliding with a goalpost in England's 1–0 defeat. Worse was to follow a month later when Salako, still only twenty-three, was carried off with badly-damaged knee ligaments in a League match against Leeds.

Salako was sent to the United States for a career-saving operation and he was ruled out for the rest of the season. It was a bitter blow after figuring strongly in Taylor's European Championship plans.

Palace manager Steve Coppell says: 'It was a shattering experience for John, but he has another ten years of his career left and we were not going to abuse him by rushing his recovery. We gave him the best opportunity possible by sending him to America and they said he needed to take off ten months.'

Salako's dazzling skills are not restricted to the wing. He began his career as a striker and Palace have the option to use him down the middle if required.

Manchester United manager Alex Ferguson has a multitude of attacking riches with Giggs, Sharpe and Kanchelskis to choose from. Giggs, nineteen in November 1992, made by far the biggest impression as United went for the League title in the 1991–92 season. United's supporters pinned their Champion-

GETTING TO GRIPS WITH THE PROBLEM

This will not appear in the schools soccer manual on the best ways to stop a flying winger. Gary Owers (Sunderland) tried it on Steve McManaman (Liverpool) and the Cup Final ref was not impressed.

The master of close control on the wing is Tony Daley, of Aston Villa and England.

ship hopes on the precocious youngster, but his verve and dashing wing play alone could not clinch the title for United in his first full season in League football.

Giggs earned favourable comparisons with George Best, the great Northern Ireland and Manchester United player of the 1960s against whom all potential United stars tend to be measured. Giggs would form a vital cog in Wales' efforts to qualify for the 1994 World Cup Finals in the United States and he would be under careful scrutiny in the 1992–93 season.

Giggs would probably not have been given his chance had Sharpe not been stuck on the sidelines after a hernia operation. He made the breakthrough in the 1990–91 season when United beat Barcelona in the European Cup Winners Cup Final.

Sharpe made his debut for England at nineteen when he came on as a second-half substitute in the European Championship qualifier against the Republic of Ireland at Wembley. Season 1992–93 promised to be especially important for him as he sought to re-establish himself at club level before contemplating a return to the international scene.

The flying Ukranian Kanchelskis completes the celebrated trio of wingers at Manchester United and his emergence shocked many. His talent was never an issue; the doubt was whether he could cope with the demands of the English League. In the event he was an unqualified success.

Defenders trailed in his wake as he sped down the line showing raw power and speed. His inclusion always gave United an extra option and much would be expected of him in his second season in England.

Elsewhere the winger is definitely back in fashion. Aston Villa's Tony Daley succeeded in making a late bid for a place in the England squad for the European Championship in Sweden. He was in dazzling form against Czechoslovakia and the CIS in the build-up to the final rounds of the Championship and Villa braced themselves for a glut of inquiries from top clubs on the Continent.

Darren Anderton made his mark with Portsmouth, the shock 1992 FA Cup semi-finalists from what was then the Second Division. They went out on penalties to eventual winners Liverpool, but he had scouts beating a path to the South Coast all season. Spurs chief Terry Venables won the race for his signature and the £1.75 million may turn out to be shrewd investment.

Meanwhile a few miles across North London, Sweden's Anders Limpar continued to woo the crowd at Arsenal. He moved to Highbury from Italians Cremonese in the summer of 1990 and was an inspirational figure in Arsenal's League title triumph a year later.

Limpar still showed magical touches the following season when Arsenal failed to mount a serious defence of their title and there would have been an outcry had he not been included in the Swedish squad for the 1992 European Championship.

There can be little doubt that the Premier League is awash with talented wingers, and supporters in England had plenty of reasons to be optimistic when the new League kicked off.

VENUES FOR 1994
WORLD CUP '94

CANADA
USA
San Francisco
Los Angeles
Detroit
Chicago
Washington D.C.
Dallas
Boston
New York
Orlando
MEXICO
Pacific Ocean

STATES NAME 9 CUP VENUES

But can they match this? ▶

WORLD CUP '94 is up and running—and the first qualifying goal was scored by an American despite the fact that the host country, as tradition decrees, has been granted automatic qualification.

Puerto Rico's skipper Mark Lugris, a restaurant manager in New York City who plays for New York Hota Barbarians, set the ball rolling on March 21, 1992, when he scored in the twenty-third minute in their Caribbean (North) qualifying game in the Dominican Republic. Puerto Rico, fielding a squad of fourteen American citizens, eventually won 2–1 and sparked the first controversy of the tournament.

All Puerto Ricans are technically US citizens holding USA passports and the Dominicans were not at all happy, arguing that the USA are in effect fielding two sides in the tournament.

The match was less than auspicious in other respects. The pitch was hard and uneven, the scoreboard didn't work, the phones didn't work and the dressing-room facilities were a shambles.

Football romantics argue that the World Cup is all about such obscure, indeed bizarre meetings, but it doesn't augur well for a competition that has

The spectacular opening ceremony of the 1990 World Cup at San Siro stadium, Milan.

Report by
BRENDAN
GALLAGHER

yet to catch the imagination. Still, there's a long way to go; in fact, there will be 582 qualifying games between 138 nations just to decide the twenty-two finalists who will join USA (as host nation) and Germany (the holders) in the finals, to be played between June 17 and July 17, 1994.

The Finals themselves are seen by many as a last-ditch effort to sell the most popular game in the World to the planet's one remaining superpower. All previous efforts have so far fallen on stony ground.

Nobody doubts that the USA has the stadia to stage World Cup '94, the ability to cater for any number of visiting fans and the communications infrastructure and expertise to cater for voracious press and media demands.

The designated stadiums are the Rose Bowl Pasadena, the Sullivan Stadium Boston, the Citrus Bowl Orlando, the Cotton Bowl Dallas, RFK Stadium Washington, Soldier Field Chicago, Giants Stadium New York, Stanford Stadium San Francisco and, most controversially of all, the indoor Pontiac Silverdome in Detroit.

The matches at the Silverdome will be the first indoor games in the World Cup Finals, something possible only on the North American continent where massive indoor stadia are very much in vogue.

Another controversial selection was that of Giants Stadium, East Rutherford, which has a maximum width of seventy-two yards, three yards shorter than the FIFA-designated minimum. A plan to build a platform and extend a 'platform pitch' into the lower seats appears to be prohibitive—so the only alternative would seem to be to use the existing narrow pitch.

FIFA are unhappy about this but insist that New York must be one of the major venues. At the announcement of the nine World Cup venues, FIFA general secretary Sepp Blatter said: 'For FIFA to bring the World Cup to the United States, the inclusion of New York is a "must". No New York, no World Cup.'

Participation statistics in the USA are at first impressive. Fifteen million Americans over the age of six play soccer at least once each year, more than 1.5 million players under the age of nineteen are registered with 90,000 youth clubs, and the number of higher education establishments fielding inter-collegiate football teams is growing all the time.

But this grass-roots interest rarely translates itself in the kind of crowds to compete with America's predominant sporting pastimes of gridiron, baseball, basketball and ice hockey. Behind the 'Big Four' everything else pales into insignificance.

But there is hope. The States' build-up to, and participation in, World Cup '90 produced a squad of players and coaches hardened in the realities of international football. Young talent is beginning to develop, witness the victory of the USA Under-17 side in a prestigious youth tournament in France in April 1992 when they beat Czechoslovakia 2–0 in the final.

Players throughout the World are beginning to examine possible American qualifications. One undeniably talented forward, Roy Wegerle of Blackburn, has opted for the States and others could follow, including the defender Tom

Roy Wegerle, seen here in QPR stripes, will be striking out for the States in '94.

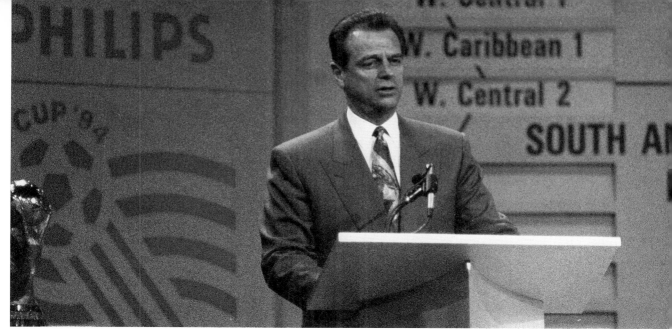

Dooley, who grew up in Germany and was a regular member of the Kaiserlautern championship side of 1991. The USA have at least become competitive at international level and are finally attracting patriotic support throughout the country, with 30,000 crowds quite common.

The home-based media have been accused of lukewarm support for the event but, in their defence, there are sound economic reasons. In 1992, an Olympic year, nothing is allowed to detract from the hype of the Barcelona Olympics for which NBC has paid $401 million for exclusive coverage rights. The Olympics are the most important international sporting event for the USA and only when they are safely out of the way will it make sense to start the build-up to World Cup '94.

The USA's biggest deficiency domestically remains the folding of the professional North American Soccer League in 1985, a League around which American soccer could have focused and found its own identity.

Various reasons were given for the folding of NASL. Negative play, high ticket prices, gross overspending by the clubs, a depressed economy, artificial turf and an ultra-businesslike approach to the game. But it all added up to one word—Economics. NASL was not economically viable.

Rising above all the doubts is Los Angeles lawyer Alan Rothenberg, President of the United States Soccer Federation, who is masterminding the staging of the World Cup.

'We will have the best of both worlds, all the passion of fans who come from abroad to support their teams, plus we will create great pageantry. We will have banners, ribbons, dances and cultural events all around the stadium. We will surprise everybody. The atmosphere will be better than anyone has seen before.'

As the Americans showed at the 1984 Olympics, they know how to stage a party. From fraught beginnings, World Cup '94 could yet prove one of the most memorable in history.

This could be a job for . . . S U P E R M A N

Otherwise known as Alan Rothenberg, mastermind of the World Cup planning for 1994.

IT'S GONNA BE A WHOLE NEW BALL GAME!

The crowds pack two of the venues for World Cup '94—but this is a different kind of ball game. Above is the Rose Bowl, Pasadena, without a roof to its name; below is the Giants Stadium, New York, where a slight problem of width has yet to be overcome.

World Cup sites and stadia . . . 1930 to 1990

WHEN the first World Championship was held in Uruguay way back in 1930, the capital, Montevideo, was big enough to accommodate thirteen teams in three stadia. In Spain in 1982, when the competition featured twenty-four finalists for the first time, no fewer than fourteen towns and seventeen stadia were involved in the contest for the World Cup title. Sweden provided twelve stadia in as many towns for sixteen teams in 1958 whereas four years later in Chile only four towns and four grounds were used. Nine cities and the same number of stadia, as planned for the 1994 World Cup in the USA, were chosen on one other previous occasion for a World Cup, namely in Germany in 1974— but for a total of only sixteen teams.

Year	Host country	Number of teams	Number of stadia		Venues
1930	Uruguay	13	3	1	Montevideo
1934	Italy	16	8	8	Rome, Trieste, Genoa, Milan, Bologna, Florence, Turin, Naples
1938	France	15	10	9	Paris (2 stadia), Reims, Strasbourg, Le Havre, Marseille, Toulouse, Bordeaux, Lille, Antibes
1950	Brazil	13	7	6	Rio de Janeiro, Belo Horizonte (2 stadia), São Paulo, Porto Alegre, Curitiba, Recife
1954	Switzerland	16	6	6	Lausanne, Geneva, Berne, Basle, Zurich, Lugano
1958	Sweden	16	12	12	Malmö, Halmstad, Helsingborg, Västeras, Norrköping, Örebro, Eskilstuna, Stockholm, Sandviken, Göteborg, Boras, Uddevalla
1962	Chile	16	4	4	Santiago, Arica, Viña del Mar, Rancagua
1966	England	16	8	7	London (2 stadia), Sheffield, Birmingham, Liverpool, Manchester, Middlesbrough, Sunderland
1970	Mexico	16	5	5	Mexico City, Puebla, Toluca, León, Guadalajara
1974	Germany FR	16	9	9	Berlin (West), Hamburg, Frankfurt, Dortmund, Gelsenkirchen, Hannover, Dusseldorf, Munich, Stuttgart
1978	Argentina	16	6	5	Buenos Aires (2 stadia), Mar del Plata, Cordoba, Rosario, Mendoza
1982	Spain	24	17	14	Madrid (2 stadia), Barcelona (2 stadia), Vigo, La Coruña, Gijon, Elche, Oviedo, Alicante, Bilbao, Valladolid, Valencia, Zaragoza, Seville (2 stadia), Malaga
1986	Mexico	24	12	8	Mexico City (3 stadia), Guadalajara (2 stadia), Toluca, Monterrey (2 stadia), Léon, Puebla, Irapuato, Queretaro
1990	Italy	24	12	12	Rome, Florence, Naples, Bari, Turin, Genoa, Milan, Bologna, Verona, Udine, Cagliari, Palermo.

HAPPY TARTAN DAYS AGAIN FOR ENGLAND CAST-OFF MARK

By GERRY COX

HATELEY of ENGLAND

MARK Hateley's favourite song could well be 'I belong to Glasgow'. The cosmopolitan striker, who is almost as well-travelled as his father Tony was, has finally decided to forsake the jet-set and settle in Glasgow.

One of Britain's wealthiest footballers, Hateley could have taken his pick of leading English clubs when he was linked with a move in the summer of 1992. But he has decided to stay with Rangers after falling for the club and its supporters—and it seems that the feeling is mutual.

After a rocky start to his career at Ibrox in 1990, Hateley became a firm favourite with the crowd and it was fitting that he scored one of the goals that won Rangers their first Scottish FA Cup for eleven years, in 1992.

That win, over Airdrieonians, clinched the club's first League and SFA Cup double since 1978 to prove once and for all that the good times were well and truly back at Ibrox.

Hateley is the latest in a long line of centre-forwards who have captured the imagination of the Rangers fans. Willie Thornton, Colin Stein and Derek Parlane were among his predecessors in Rangers' illustrious past. And Hateley has a colourful history himself. He has experienced football's highs and lows since shooting to prominence as a teenager with Coventry in the early 1980s.

The highs have been vertiginous—he was England's World Cup centre-forward, idolised by the fans of AC Milan and living the luxurious lifestyle that comes with million-pound deals—but the lows have been cruel. Injuries, sporadic loss of form and exile from international football after he thought he had estabished himself as England's regular centre-forward.

After winning thirty-one caps, Hateley was discarded in 1988 when England crashed out of the European Championship finals. In another cruel twist, he was given brief hope of resurrecting his international career in Czechoslovakia in March 1992, only to be dumped after one match.

Yet throughout his career, he has proved that he can score goals in the toughest leagues in the world and at international level, with nine for England.

Initially, it was the name that aroused interest. At the start of his career, Mark Hateley had to live with the suffix 'son of Tony' because of his famous

father who scored goals galore for Notts County, Chelsea, Liverpool and Aston Villa in the 1960s.

Early in his career, Mark said: 'Those words made me squirm. Whenever I saw that phrase in match reports, it made me think the Press only mentioned me because of my father.'

Having started out at Coventry, another of his father's former clubs, Mark was soon making headlines in his own way after moving to Portsmouth. His twenty-two goals for Second Division Pompey earned him an England call-up, and he scored on his full debut, against Brazil in the Maracana Stadium.

John Barnes's amazing solo goal in that 2–0 win may have stolen the headlines but it was Hateley who was off to Italian giants AC Milan a few weeks later for nearly £1 million. Fears about the twenty-two-year-old's ability to cope were soon dispelled when he made a dream start, scoring five goals in his first six games. The fans loved his aggressive and determined style and nicknamed him 'Attila'.

After scoring the winner in an intense local derby against Internazionale, Hateley became a hero to half of Milan. When he walked into a restaurant, fans would stand and applaud. Then a cartilage operation disrupted his season and the goals dried up for a while. He also fell out with club officials, especially president Guiseppe Farina, although the Milanese fans refused to join in the criticism at first.

But 1986 was a bad year. He was dropped by England midway through the World Cup finals, and his love affair with the Milan crowd started to turn sour on his return to Italy. 'I thought I was unlucky to be left out of the World Cup side and was very disappointed,' he said. 'I had scored four goals in five games leading up to the finals and had got most of the goals to get us there.'

Eventually, in 1988, he was transferred for £1 million to Monaco, where he linked up with Glenn Hoddle and started rattling in goals once again as the side won the French Championship. But injury struck again, and with his family homesick for Britain, Hateley finally joined Rangers in 1990, having turned them down three years earlier.

'I missed playing in front of big, passionate crowds,' he said. 'In Italy, I

An all-England international line-up on a foreign field: Glenn Hoddle, Trevor Francis, Mark Hateley. Result: Monaco 0, Rangers 0.

was used to 75,000 sell-outs, but at Monaco we were playing to 5,000 in some matches.'

He certainly found the big-match atmosphere with Rangers but was not an instant success. He failed to impress fans and manager Graeme Souness in his early months and was dropped.

He managed only ten goals in his first season and suffered the ignominy of being sent off in a 2–0 defeat by arch-rivals Celtic. But with typical determination, he fought his way back, scoring the two goals that beat Aberdeen on the final day of the season to clinch the championship.

With his injury problems behind him, Hateley is playing as well as ever. Not only is he big and strong, he is quick and mobile and as former team-mate Ray Wilkins points out: 'He is as good as any striker of his type in Britain.'

However, after failing to make the England squad for the 1992 European Championship finals, Hateley pledged to devote all his time and energy to playing for Rangers. That can only be Rangers' gain and England's loss.

MARK'S THE MAN WITH CUP-WINNING WAYS...

Mark Hateley shows the style that helped Rangers to win the Scottish Cup in 1992 for the first time for eleven years. His name was on the scoresheet.

ANOTHER MARKSMAN WITH THE CUP-WINNING TOUCH

Ian Rush has that goalscoring knack on Wembley occasions, and he was on the mark for Liverpool in the FA Cup Final of '92. Hence the celebration here with Michael Thomas.

A MIGHTY TRIO IN HIGHBURY'S HALL OF FAME

THE 1991–92 season saw the death of three of the greatest players in Arsenal's history — Cliff Bastin, Joe Hulme and Jack Kelsey.

CLIFF ('*Boy*') BASTIN and Hulme played on opposite wings in the all-conquering Arsenal side of the 1930s. Bastin was a teenage prodigy who won every honour in the game by the time he was twenty-one and still ranks as one of British football's finest forwards.

Signed from his native Exeter at the age of seventeen, he won an FA Cup winners medal at eighteen, a League Championship medal at nineteen and an England cap at twenty in 1932. The following season he scored thirty-three goals from the wing, a League record that still stands.

Bastin had been converted from a good inside-forward to a great left-winger by his idol Herbert Chapman, although he played thirteen of his twenty-one England games, during which he scored twelve goals, at inside-left.

When he retired in 1946, after 396 games and 178 goals for Arsenal, it was discovered that he had been almost completely deaf for ten years. He lived in quiet retirement in Devon until his death at the age of seventy-nine.

During Bastin's career at Highbury, Arsenal won the League five times and the FA Cup twice.

Most of those triumphs were shared by **JOE HULME**, the right-winger who

Flying wings and ever thirsty for G-O-A-L-S

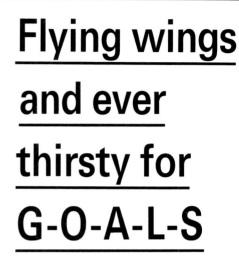

Old-time memories are stirred by these pictures of Joe Hulme (above) and Cliff Bastin (right), both high-speed wingers with a thirst for goals. Joe is pictured above with the old leather ball and Pat Beasley, also ex-Arsenal, as they prepare for Huddersfield Town's 1938 Cup Final at Wembley.

was considered the quickest man in British football when Chapman signed him from Blackburn Rovers in 1927. He once ran in the Powderhall Sprint, the Scottish professional race held each New Year's Day.

Hulme was one of that rare breed of top footballers who also played first-class cricket, batting for Middlesex, but he was more famous as a footballer, winning nine England caps between 1927 and 1936 and many other honours.

Arsenal's forward line of Hulme, Jack, Lambert, James and Bastin was considered by many to be among the greatest attacks in British football history. Joe himself scored 108 goals in 333 League games for Arsenal.

He became the first player to appear in five FA Cup Finals at Wembley, a record subsequently equalled but never beaten. The last of them was for Huddersfield Town in 1938, his final first-class appearance.

After the war, Joe switched allegiance when he moved across North London to become manager of Tottenham Hotspur, Arsenal's great rivals. His three years at White Hart Lane were not his happiest—he was rumoured to be earning less than his players—but he helped lay the foundation for Arthur Rowe's great 'push and run' side that won the Second Division in 1950 and League Championship in 1951.

In the 1950s and '60s Joe moved into sports journalism working for *The People* until he retired in the 1970s. He died at the age of eighty-seven.

Forever Arsenal

Jack Kelsey, an Arsenal servant for 38 years.

JACK KELSEY, who played in a later era at Highbury, was one of the club's great goalkeepers and was considered by some supporters to be the finest in Arsenal's history.

The strongly-built Welshman got off to the worst possible start, letting in five goals on his Arsenal debut in 1951 after being signed from Swansea junior club Winch Wen. But he went on to win a League Championship medal in 1952–53, his only prize with Arsenal although he was first-choice 'keeper for nearly ten years.

He established himself as the Welsh national goalkeeper in 1954, going on to win forty-one caps and play in two World Cups.

In the first, in 1958, he was one of the stars as Wales fought heroically before going down 1–0 to Brazil and the eighteen-year-old Pelé. His second appearance came in 1962 and marked the end of his career. After injuring his back badly against Brazil, he never recovered and retired to take over the running of Arsenal's club shop.

Kelsey finally ended a long association with Highbury when he retired from his post as commercial manager in 1989. He died from cancer in May 1992 at the age of sixty-three.

Stan's partner to the end . . .

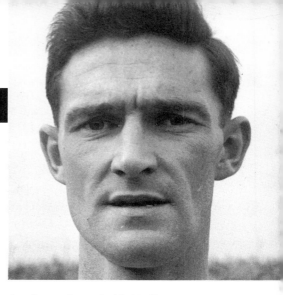

Jackie Mudie, seventeen times capped for Scotland, was the chief supplier of openings for Matthews and Mortensen.

JACKIE MUDIE was a survivor of an age when a footballer was judged mostly by what he could do with the ball at his feet.

Speed, stamina and physique were important but the real money was paid for artistry. The crowds came, in their eighty-thousands, less to see a win from the home team, more to see Matthews or Finney or Shackleton.

Mudie was a small Scottish inside-forward who created openings for strong centre-forwards or wingers by his control, tactical invention and passing skills. An attacking midfielder would be his description today, for Mudie, by wriggling past heavy defenders on the muddy fields of the early Fifties, leather ball tied to his boots, could also score goals.

His famous days were with Blackpool where he fitted exactly in between Stanley Matthews at outside-right and Stan Mortensen at centre-forward. He also played seventeen times for Scotland at a time when every kid in Scotland grew up playing the game and the dark blue cap was worth an earldom.

Mudie was an integral part of a great Blackpool team whose tangerine shirts lit up briefly but gloriously the austere days of the post-war decade. With as many as nine internationals in the team, Blackpool would arrive in London in style and stay at a four-star hotel. Porters, commissionaires and head waiters would snap to attention when their manager Joe Smith boomed out across a crowded lobby: 'This is Blackpool Football Club.'

Mudie was also the catalyst in one of football's most extraordinary stories. He was thirty-one when Stoke City, on the verge of relegation to the Third Division, pestered Blackpool to release him. Stoke's young manager, Tony Waddington, given £5,000 to save the club, eventually signed Mudie for £3,000. 'There was never a better investment,' Waddington said.

Stoke pulled ten men back behind the ball, an amazing manoeuvre in 1961, leaving Mudie upfield: 'He scored a few goals for us that season but every one brought a win and we stayed up. Jackie was five foot nothing, a lightweight. You could sum up his ability in three words: skill, skill and skill.'

Mudie went on to score thirty-two goals in eighty-nine appearances for Stoke and was the first purchase in a gallery of artists Waddington brought to the Victoria Ground in the next fifteen years: Dennis Viollet, Jimmy McIlroy, Peter

Dobing, Roy Vernon, Terry Conroy, George Eastham, John Mahoney, Jimmy Greenhoff, Alan Hudson.

It was Mudie who helped persuade Matthews to return to Stoke, the move that swept the club back to the First Division. Mudie, on a coaching course with Matthews in Canada, rang Waddington to say: 'The old bugger can still do it, Tony.' Mudie and Matthews were reunited briefly at Port Vale and the pair remained almost inseparable until the Scotsman's death. It was rare to see one without the other and minutes in their company could be turned magical by the telling of tales, always humorous, often self-deprecatory, rarely malicious, usually a sad reminder of how modern football has lost the ability to laugh at itself.

Mudie was a mostly shy and self-effacing man in public, blossoming within the team environment. Waddington again:

'He was a great man in the dressing-room, using his experience and sense of humour to settle down the younger lads without upsetting the older players. He served Blackpool and Stoke City magnificently. It was perhaps in his nature that he should not be as publicised as many of his contemporaries, being quite content to spend most of his career in Stan's shadow, but in my reckoning Jackie Mudie will always be one of the truly great players, his professionalism being more easily recognised inside the team and on the field rather than by the spectators.

'He was a gentleman, a smashing lad who went through a lot of pain and discomfort in his last illness but he and Brenda were still able to joke about it when I last spoke to them.' — **Derek Hodgson.**

● *Our thanks to The Independent for permission to reproduce this appreciation of John Knight ('Jackie') Mudie, who died in March 1992 at the age of sixty-one.*

THE FINEST HEADER

WILLIE THORNTON, who has died at the age of seventy-one, was a goal-scoring legend at Glasgow Rangers. A dynamic centre-forward, Thornton scored 188 goals in 303 matches between 1936 and 1954 and was considered the finest header of a ball in Rangers' history. He was also one of the most skilful forwards in Scotland and would surely have won more than his seven caps had his career not been interrupted by the Second World War.

Spotted playing for Winchburgh Albion, Thornton made his debut for Rangers at sixteen and went on to form a fearsome partnership with winger Willie Waddell. He was leading scorer in each of the first six seasons after the war.

Thornton was named Scotland's Player of the Year in 1952 before retiring in 1954 to go into management. After spells at Dundee and Partick Thistle, he joined the coaching staff at Ibrox where he linked up again with Waddell in 1970.

Thornton's bravery was not confined to the football field, for he was awarded the Military Medal while serving with the Duke of Atholl's Highlanders in Italy during the war.

NICE ONE, OUR CYRIL

CYRIL KNOWLES will be remembered forever in football folklore as the man who inspired the top-twenty hit 'Nice One, Cyril' in the early 1970s, but to a generation of Tottenham fans, he was the fast-raiding left-back who carried forward the club's traditions of excitement, skill and entertainment.

It was only because of Terry Cooper's excellence in that position that Knowles did not win more than his four full England caps. In another era, he would surely have been first choice for his country with his ferocious tackling, swift counter-attacking and stunning free-kicks.

In those respects, Cyril was not unlike Stuart Pearce, England's latest captain. The major difference was that whereas Pearce is a dour figure, Knowles was one of football's great characters, with a smile on his face and a rapport with the crowd.

Born in the Yorkshire mining village of Fitzwilliam, he joined Spurs from Middlesbrough in 1964 for £45,000. He helped Spurs win the FA Cup in 1967, the League Cup in 1971 and 1973 and the UEFA Cup in 1972. A serious knee injury in 1973 led to his eventual retirement from playing in 1976 after more than 500 games for Tottenham.

A promising career in management beckoned, first at Darlington and then Torquay, with whom he won promotion from the Fourth Division. After repeating the feat with Hartlepool, he suffered a brain tumour and died at the early age of forty-eight.

A memorial game between some of the great names from Spurs and Arsenal was an emotional occasion and a fitting tribute to one of North London's favourite adopted sons. It was, to borrow a phrase, a 'nice one, Cyril'. —**Gerry Cox.**

EXPLOSIVE SKILLS

JUAN GOMEZ 'JUANITO', who was killed in a car crash on his way home from Real Madrid's UEFA Cup semi-final tie against Torino in 1992, was one of Spain's most famous players. An inspirational right-winger, his temper often matched his explosive skills.

Born in Fuengirola, he played for Atletico Madrid and Burgos but it was at Real Madrid where he made his name. He was part of the Real side which dominated Spanish football in the late 1970s and had its fair share of success in European competition, winning UEFA Cup honours in 1985 and 1986.

Juanito formed a devastating attacking partnership with Carlos Santillana and scored ninety-four League goals for the Castillian club, including seventeen as top scorer in season 1983–84. On the international front, he won thirty-four caps for Spain and played at the 1978 and 1982 World Cups as well as the 1980 European Championship.

He went into coaching on his retirement from playing and his ambition was, one day, to return as manager of his beloved Real. —**John Price.**

Alan Davies, who died tragically, seen here in the glory days with Manchester United.

ALAN DAVIES, Swansea winger and former Welsh international, was found dead in his car at a beauty spot just outside Swansea in February 1992. He was only thirty.

Davies came to national prominence when, aged twenty-one and after just a handful of first-team appearances, he played a starring role in Manchester United's 1983 FA Cup Final win over Brighton, whom they beat 4–0 after a replay. But he was unable to fulfil that early promise, largely due to injury which dogged him throughout his career.

Davies, who won eleven Welsh caps, also played for Newcastle, Charlton, Carlisle and Bradford before his second spell with Swansea.

GUNNAR GREN was one of Sweden's greatest players. An inside-forward, he was an Olympic gold medal winner with Sweden in the 1948 Games at Wembley. A year later he moved to Italy, where he formed part of Milan's legendary Gre-No-Li inside-forward trio with fellow countrymen Gunnar Nordahl and Nils Liedholm.

He returned home to help Sweden in the 1958 World Cup. They reached the final only to lose 5–2 against a Pelé-inspired Brazil. Later, Gren ran a souvenir shop at the Ullevi Stadium in his native Gothenburg. He was seventy-one.

MIKHAIL MESHKI, a member of the victorious Soviet Union side at the European Championship in 1960, died aged fifty-three. An outside-left, he was one half of a potent wing attack at Dynamo Tbilisi with Slava Metrevelli. He helped the Georgian club to the Soviet League title in 1964 and won thirty-five international caps.

THEO LASEROMS was in the outstanding Feyenoord side which lifted the 1970 European Cup after a 2–1 final defeat of Celtic in Milan. Capped six times by Holland, he also had spells in Belgium and the United States with Ghent and Pittsburgh Pirates respectively. Later he went into coaching before his death in his home town of Zwolle at the age of fifty-one.

WALTER ZEMAN, one of the finest European goalkeepers of the 1950s, was nicknamed the 'Glasgow Tiger' after an outstanding display when Austria beat Scotland 1–0 at Hampden Park in 1950. He made forty-four appearances for Austria between 1947–60 and played for the World XI in the 4–4 draw against England at Wembley in 1953. He was sixty-four.

CONCETTO LO BELLO, Italy's most famous referee from 1953 to 1974, died in his native Syracuse, aged sixty-seven. He took charge of 328 Italian First Division matches and ninety-three international games. His other international engagements included the 1966 World Cup, the 1960 Olympic Games, the 1969 and 1970 Champions' Cup Finals, the 1967 Cup-Winners Cup Final and 1974 UEFA Cup Final.